Smithsonian National Air and Space Museum

MILESTONES OF FLIGHT

FROM HOT-AIR BALLOONS TO SPACESHIPONE

★ ★

TIM GROVE

ABRAMS BOOKS FOR YOUNG READERS ★ NEW YORK

Library of Congress Cataloging-in-Publication Data

Names: Grove, Tim—author. | National Air and Space Museum.
Title: Milestones of flight : from hot-air balloons to SpaceShipOne /
by Tim Grove.
Description: New York : Abrams Books for Young Readers, [2016] | Includes
bibliographical references and index. | Audience: 10–14.
Identifiers: LCCN 2015033040 | ISBN 9781419720031
Subjects: LCSH: Aeronautics—History—Chronology—Juvenile literature. |
Astronautics—History—Chronology—Juvenile literature.
Classification: LCC TL515 .G76 2016 | DDC 629.109—dc23
LC record available at http://lccn.loc.gov/2015033040

Text copyright © 2016 The Smithsonian National Air and Space Museum

For illustration credits, see page 99.

Book design by Sara Corbett

Printed and bound in China
10 9 8 7 6 5 4 3 2 1

Abrams Books for Young Readers are available at special
discounts when purchased in quantity for premiums and promotions
as well as fundraising or educational use. Special editions
can also be created to specification. For details, contact
specialsales@abramsbooks.com or the address below.

ABRAMS
THE ART OF BOOKS SINCE 1949

115 West 18th Street
New York, NY 10011
www.abramsbooks.com

CONTENTS

EARTH

25 26

4

4

1

7 5

2 6

13

MOON

22

1 FIRST HOT AIR BALLOON (FRANCE)

2 WRIGHT FLYER (KITTYHAWK, NC)

3 CURTISS JN-4, THE "JENNY"

4 DOUGLAS WORLD CRUISER

5 GODDARD ROCKET INVENTED (MASSACHUSETTS)

6 FLIGHT OF THE *SPIRIT OF ST. LOUIS*

7 FULL SCALE WIND TUNNEL BUILT IN VIRGINA

8 DOUGLAS DC-3

9 UAVS

10 BELL XP-59A AIRACOMET WHITTLE AND JUMO 004B ENGINES

MILESTONES OF FLIGHT

NEPTUNE

SATURN

URANUS

24 MARS

18 VENUS

23 JUPITER

EARTH

MERCURY

SUN

11 BELL X-1, *GLAMOROUS GLENNIS*

12 BOEING 367-80, "DASH 80"

13 SPUTNIK 1 AND EXPLORER 1 ENTER OUTER SPACE FROM RUSSIA AND AMERICA

14 NORTH AMERICAN X-15

15 DISCOVERER/CORONA

16 TELSTAR

17 MERCURY *FRIENDSHIP 7*

18 *MARINER 2*

19 LOCKHEED SR-71 BLACKBIRD

20 *GEMINI IV*

21 IMAGINATION AND THE *STAR TREK* STARSHIP *ENTERPRISE*

22 FIRST FLIGHT TO THE MOON

23 *PIONEER 10/11* TRANSMITS PHOTOS OF JUPITER

24 *VIKING* LANDER EXPLORES MARS

25 SPACE SHUTTLE DISCOVERY

26 HUBBLE SPACE TELESCOPE TAKES PHOTOS BEYOND OUR SOLAR SYSTEM

27 SPACESHIPONE

INTRODUCTION

★ ★ ★

WHAT WOULD
IT BE LIKE TO FLY? HUMANS HAVE LONG
LOOKED AT BIRDS AND WONDERED. BUT THE
PULL OF GRAVITY MAKES IT HARD TO LEAVE EARTH.

The first human-made object to defy Earth's gravity and fly was a kite. Kites were invented in China more than a thousand years ago. Today kite flying is still popular around the world. It's fun to take a brightly colored kite outside on a windy day, give it some air, and watch it climb into the sky. A skillful kite flier can make a kite soar and dive and weave.

Not until 1783 did humans figure out how *they* could take flight. Two brothers in France sent the first humans skyward. Their experiments with hot-air balloons changed the way people viewed the world. More than a hundred years later, two brothers in the United States solved the puzzle of controlled flight and invented the airplane.

The story of humanity's quest to fly is told in the many objects, drawings, documents, photos, and other evidence that have been preserved and collected in

FLYING A KITE

① SMITHSONIAN NATIONAL AIR AND SPACE
MUSEUM, WASHINGTON, D.C.

② CHINESE KITE FROM THE FIRST GROUP
OF AIR-RELATED OBJECTS COLLECTED BY THE
SMITHSONIAN.

museums. The Smithsonian National Air and Space Museum in Washington, D.C., holds the largest collection of air- and space-related objects in the world. Therefore, it's a good starting place to learn about how we got to where we are today. The first flight objects that the Smithsonian collected were kites. The Chinese delegation at the Philadelphia Centennial Exposition in 1876 presented the Smithsonian with an almost fifty-foot-long dragon kite and several other kites, and they became the basis for the museum's unparalleled flight collection.

Each milestone described in this book was an important moment or innovation in the history of flight. Many, but not all, led to a major advancement in flight. The list includes some of the most iconic objects in the Smithsonian's collection. Most of them happen to be American, mainly because the United States has been a leader in flight from the beginning. But many other countries have mastered the air and contributed to the story of human flight as well. By no means is this a comprehensive list.

Milestones of Flight gathers some of the most significant airplanes, rockets, and spacecraft in history. These soaring machines tell us a lot about our world. They speak of ingenuity and courage, war and peace, and politics and power, as well as society and culture. In many ways these milestones of flight have made our planet seem smaller and the universe appear larger. They have transformed our world.

FIRST ASCENT OF THE MONTGOLFIER BROTHERS' BALLOON ON NOVEMBER 21, 1783, FROM THE GARDEN OF THE CHÂTEAU DE LA MUETTE, PARIS.

BALLOONING

WHAT HAPPENED

WHEN A SHEEP, A DUCK, AND A ROOSTER FLOATED UP IN A HOT-AIR BALLOON? BELIEVE IT OR NOT, THEIR TRIP LED TO HUMAN FLIGHT.

The first time humans escaped Earth's gravity was in a brightly colored hot-air balloon. Although people in Asian cultures had launched small hot-air balloons centuries before, the first ride into the sky wasn't until 1783. In September of that year two French brothers—Joseph-Michel and Jacques Étienne Montgolfier, who were papermakers—experimented with flight by placing a sheep, a duck, and a rooster into a gondola attached to a balloon that was made of paper and fabric. Up they went! This occurred near Paris, at the Palace of Versailles, with King Louis XVI and Queen Marie Antoinette watching. After eight minutes the balloon and its passengers landed safely. They had traveled two miles! Two months later, on November 21, the brothers sent two human passengers up in an untethered balloon. They were the first humans to fly.

The brothers flew their balloons many other times. Crowds gathered to watch. Benjamin Franklin and other Americans who were in Paris at the time to negotiate a peace treaty with Britain witnessed the balloon flights. Ten years later balloons came to America. The first flight was launched from a prison yard in Philadelphia, and President George Washington and four future presidents were watching. Washington sent a letter in the balloon for delivery to the owner of the property wherever the balloon landed. Was this the first airmail?

Before hot-air balloons, human beings had never flown. Flying in balloons and seeing Earth from a new perspective changed people's thoughts on geography, science, politics, and society. Balloons represented freedom of movement. A person in a balloon flew where the wind blew him. He did not have to follow a road or a river. From a balloon one could not see political boundaries. The precise lines where one country ended and another began became blurred.

Ballooning caught the imagination of the public. Balloon-inspired hairstyles and clothing became all the rage in the final years of the eighteenth century. Craftsmen and merchants produced jewelry, hats, fans, snuffboxes, matchboxes, needle cases, dinnerware, wallpaper, birdcages, chandeliers, clocks, furniture, and a host of other balloon-themed objects to attract the eye (and open the pocketbook) of customers. The fad lasted into the 1800s.

The techniques of lighter-than-air flight that were discovered centuries ago remain the guiding principles of ballooning today. This type of flight grew out of the Scientific Revolution, a period of great advances. Studies of the atmosphere during the 1600s led to Robert Boyle's description of the relationship between volume, temperature, and pressure and a new understanding of air. This inspired the possibility of lighter-than-air flight. Then in the 1700s chemists began identifying the gases in the atmosphere. Once

A FASHIONABLE FRENCHWOMAN FROM THE LATE 1700S.

hydrogen was isolated, the idea of filling a bag with this light gas followed. It was lighter than other gases in the air and would therefore float. The inventors of the balloon based their work on a new concept called the "scientific method": Educated guesses are made and then tested.

Very soon after the first flight, people recognized the balloon's potential military value. From a balloon, soldiers could spy on the enemy. The army of revolutionary France first employed observation balloons at the battles of Fleurus and Charleroi in 1794.

Professor Thaddeus Lowe (1832–1913) was an American pioneer in ballooning and is considered the father of aerial reconnaissance in the United States. At the age of eighteen he attended a chemistry lecture about lighter-than-air gases. He became fascinated with balloons and eventually began offering rides in tethered balloons at fairs. By the late 1850s Lowe was known for building balloons. He even dreamed of flying one across the Atlantic Ocean. One of his balloons, named the *City of New York*, measured 103 feet in diameter. During a

THE NEW AIR-SHIP "CITY OF NEW YORK."—[See Page 609.]

THIS WOODCUT ILLUSTRATION SHOWS THADDEUS LOWE'S *CITY OF NEW YORK*, DESIGNED TO CROSS THE ATLANTIC, IN 1859.

PROFESSOR THADDEUS LOWE DURING THE CIVIL WAR.

test flight, Lowe traveled from Cincinnati to South Carolina: The wind blew him 400 miles off his planned course to Washington, D.C.

While the start of the Civil War ended his quest to cross the Atlantic, it brought another opportunity. At the suggestion of the head of the Smithsonian Institution, Lowe gave a demonstration to President Abraham Lincoln, showing how the Union army could use balloons to track enemy movements and how balloons

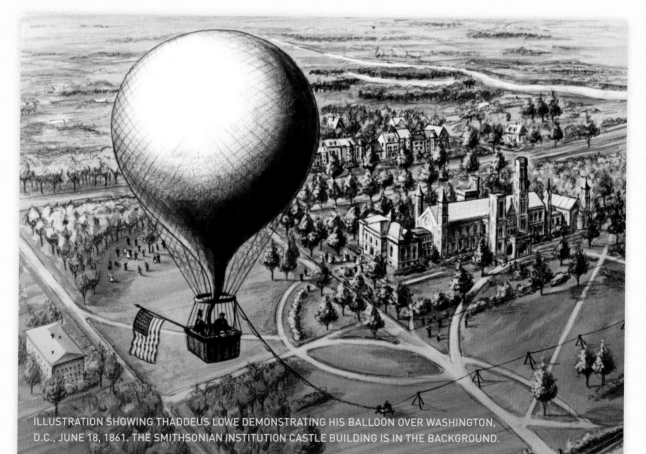

ILLUSTRATION SHOWING THADDEUS LOWE DEMONSTRATING HIS BALLOON OVER WASHINGTON, D.C., JUNE 18, 1861. THE SMITHSONIAN INSTITUTION CASTLE BUILDING IS IN THE BACKGROUND.

could help mapmakers draw more accurate maps. (Today the National Air and Space Museum in Washington, D.C., stands near the spot where Lowe gave his demonstration.) Lincoln approved the first military aeronautical unit in U.S. history, and in 1862 Lowe launched the first military balloon flight for the Union army.

Military forces around the world soon incorporated Lowe's aerial reconnaissance techniques. But Lowe was sick of war. He moved on to other interests and never did attempt a balloon flight across the Atlantic Ocean. That feat wasn't accomplished until more than a hundred years later, in 1978, when a balloon named the *Double Eagle II* flew from Maine to Paris in six days.

Vehicles of flight have changed a great deal since the first humans ascended in an untethered balloon. But hot-air balloons continue to offer humans a look at Earth from a different perspective.

THADDEUS LOWE IN A BALLOON DURING THE BATTLE OF FAIR OAKS, ATTRIBUTED TO PHOTOGRAPHER MATTHEW BRADY.

WRIGHT FLYER

MANY PEOPLE
WOULD SAY THAT THE MOST IMPORTANT
MILESTONE IN THE HISTORY OF FLIGHT OCCURRED
ON DECEMBER 17, 1903, WHEN TWO BROTHERS
FROM OHIO FLEW THE FIRST AIRPLANE.

To be specific, it was the first powered, heavier-than-air machine to achieve controlled, sustained flight with a pilot on board. Many others throughout history had tried to fly, but they hadn't been able to figure out how to control their airplane and stay in the air. Finally, after many people built funny-looking flying machines that didn't work, Orville and Wilbur Wright figured out the components and built one that did work. *Every* airplane since the 1903 Wright Flyer has incorporated the same basic design elements! Yet the

WILBUR (*LEFT*) AND ORVILLE WRIGHT
SEATED ON PORCH STEPS OF FAMILY HOME
IN DAYTON, OHIO, CIRCA JUNE 1909.

Wright brothers didn't set out to change the world; they just wanted to solve a puzzle.

Orville and Wilbur both had an engineer's mind. They asked lots of questions and were fascinated with how machines work. Between 1899 and 1905 they conducted a program of aeronautical research and experimentation that led to a practical airplane. They began by gathering data from other researchers. They wrote to the Smithsonian Institution requesting reference materials. Then they isolated three specific challenges that needed to be solved:

THE LETTER THE WRIGHT BROTHERS WROTE TO THE SMITHSONIAN INSTITUTION ON MAY 30, 1899, ASKING FOR INFORMATION ABOUT FLIGHT.

❶ Lift—what surfaces (wings) would carry the vehicle off the ground and keep it in the air?

❷ Balance and control—how could a person control the vehicle?

❸ Propulsion—what would keep the flight going?

They decided to experiment first with balance and control. Their experience building bicycles, which they sold in their own shop, proved worthwhile. James Howard Means, editor of the journal *Aeronautical Annual*, published an article in 1896 called "Wheeling and Flying" in which he made a connection between bicycles and flight. He wrote: "It is not uncommon for the cyclist ... to remark [that] Wheeling [a term for riding a bicycle] is just like flying! ... To learn to wheel one must learn to balance; to learn to fly one must learn to balance." A bicycle was an unstable but controllable machine. Why couldn't an airplane work the same way?

In thinking about control and lift, the Wright brothers realized that if they could figure out how to change the airflow over one of the wings, it would create a difference in lift between the two wings. Control of airflow could both maintain balance and cause the plane to turn. But how could they change the airflow? One day Wilbur was absentmindedly twisting a cardboard box for a bicycle inner tube as he chatted with a customer. He observed that even when he applied a considerable twist, the box retained its stiffness along its length. It occurred to him that the same principle could be applied to a set of wings. He had just invented a concept called "wing warping."

To test their theories about control, the Wright brothers built and flew a biplane kite with a five-foot wingspan. With the successful testing of the kite, they were ready for experimenting with a large glider, complete with a pilot. First they needed to find a place to fly with steady winds, wide-open space, and, ideally, soft landing material. They found this at Kitty Hawk, a small fishing village on the barrier islands of North Carolina. Sand was the perfect surface for a soft landing.

SIDE VIEW OF DAN TATE (*LEFT*) AND WILBUR WRIGHT FLYING THE 1902 GLIDER AS A KITE AT KITTY HAWK, NORTH CAROLINA.

Starting in 1900, they built a series of three gliders over a three-year period. Each year they returned to Kitty Hawk and tested a new one. The gliders helped them test balance and control, as well as learn how to fly. Because gliders have no engine, they rely on gravity and air to stay in the air. Later, in 1901, back in Ohio, the Wrights built a wind tunnel to measure the force of lift and drag acting on a wing. They conducted tests on as many as 200 models of different wing shapes!

After making hundreds of successful

flights in their third glider in 1902, the brothers designed and built a larger airplane. They traveled to North Carolina in the fall of 1903 determined to add an engine and fly a powered airplane. By now they had overcome many of the major obstacles through a disciplined engineering process of calculated experimentation.

The first flight took place on December 17, with Orville at the controls. He flew 120 feet in twelve seconds. They made three more flights that day, and on the last one Wilbur flew 852 feet in fifty-nine seconds. Then a wind gust caught them by surprise and flipped the aircraft over while it was on the ground, and it never flew again. The Wright brothers called their first powered airplane the "Flyer."

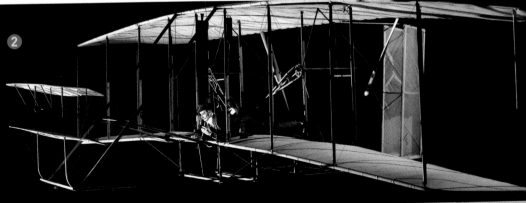

❶ WITH ORVILLE WRIGHT AT THE CONTROLS AND WILBUR WRIGHT MID-STRIDE (*RIGHT*), THE 1903 WRIGHT FLYER MAKES ITS FIRST FLIGHT AT KITTY HAWK, DECEMBER 17, 1903.

❷ THE ORIGINAL WRIGHT FLYER IS ON DISPLAY AT THE NATIONAL AIR AND SPACE MUSEUM.

CURTISS JN-4, THE "JENNY"

GLENN CURTISS

WAS ANOTHER AVIATION PIONEER. LIKE THE WRIGHT BROTHERS, HE STARTED WITH BICYCLES. HE BUILT THEM AND RACED THEM, THEN SWITCHED TO MOTORCYCLES AND FINALLY TO AIRPLANES.

He won a race at the world's first international air meet, held in France in 1909. The following year he made the first long-distance flight in the United States, from Albany, New York, to New York City. In 1911, Curtiss received U.S. pilot's license number 1 from the Aero Club of America. (Because the first licenses were issued in alphabetical order, Orville Wright received license number 5.) That same year Curtiss started the Curtiss Aeroplane Company, which built one of the most beloved U.S. airplanes of all time.

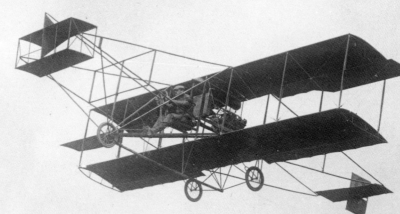

GLENN CURTISS. CURTISS FLYING HIS HERRING-CURTISS NO. 2, THE "REIMS RACER," AT REIMS, FRANCE, AUGUST 22–29, 1909.

It was the first airplane that many Americans saw close-up, and it was affectionately called the "Jenny" because of its model number, JN-4. ("JN," followed by an open-topped 4 that looked like a *Y*). The Curtiss Aeroplane Company originally built the Jenny as a training airplane for the U.S. Army. During World War I (1914–18) it produced more than 6,000 of them. More than 90 percent of the American pilots who flew in the war learned to fly in this basic but sturdy airplane. After the war the Jenny appeared in Hollywood movies and in air circuses (called "barnstorming shows") all around the country. Often a person's first ride in an airplane was in a Jenny.

Even though the first Jenny flew in 1916, its popularity extended into the 1930s. After World War I ended in 1918, the plane became the foundation of postwar civil aviation. The military sold thousands of surplus planes at bargain prices to private owners. One option for former military pilots who were still eager to fly was joining a circus—an air circus. These traveling air shows featured daring airplane stunts, including wing walking. The Jenny was the perfect plane for this, because it was slow and steady. But when needed, it could also fly up to 75 miles per hour.

One of the most famous pilots in the world—Charles Lindbergh, the first person to fly solo across the Atlantic Ocean—flew a Jenny. He purchased one for $500 in 1923 after he'd taken some flying lessons. It was the first plane he ever owned. He

WING-WALKER ORMER LOCKLEAR HANGING BY HIS KNEES
IN A BARNSTORMING SHOW, CIRCA 1919–20.

soon began flying his Jenny solo and then joined a barnstorming group and flew as "Daredevil Lindbergh." Lindbergh eventually sold his Jenny to a student in Iowa. Almost fifty years later the plane was found stored in a pig barn. Because of Lindbergh's fame, it was restored and is now on display at the Cradle of Aviation Museum in Garden City, New York.

Many other famous pilots flew these planes. Amelia Earhart, the first woman to fly solo across the Atlantic Ocean, learned to fly in a Jenny, and Bessie Coleman, the first African American to earn an international pilot's license, flew one in air shows.

People across the United States witnessed barnstorming shows, but the Jenny gained even more exposure through Hollywood movies. Americans flocked to see the thrilling cinematic air stunts. The Jenny helped make aviation popular and introduced an entire country to flying.

And the Jenny had one more important role to play: It ushered in the age of airmail. On the morning of May 15, 1918, two airmail pilots in Jennys took off, one from Washington, D.C., and the other from the Belmont Park racetrack on Long Island, New York. In Philadelphia, the halfway point, they were expected to meet, exchange mailbags, and then return to their starting points. At least that was the plan. The pilot from Washington, however, promptly got lost. Navigating with a road map and a faulty compass, he went in the opposite direction, ending up in Waldorf, Maryland, south of Washington. On landing, he flipped his Jenny, damaging it and ending his flight. But the mail arrived from New York, and the age of flying the mail had begun.

The Post Office Department printed a stamp to honor the inauguration of airmail delivery. The stamp featured a Jenny, but one sheet of the stamps was printed upside down by mistake. The "inverted Jenny" has become one of the most valuable of all stamps. Today a few of these mistakes still exist, and they are worth a lot of money!

MAJOR REUBEN H. FLEET (*LEFT*), HOLDING AN AVIATION MAP, LOOKS AT HIS HAMILTON WRISTWATCH PRIOR TO THE FIRST FLIGHT OF THE WASHINGTON TO PHILADELPHIA AIRPLANE MAIL SERVICE, MAY 15, 1918. LIEUTENANT GEORGE L. BOYLE, THE PILOT, LOOKS ON. THE MAP DIDN'T HELP—BOYLE ENDED UP IN WALDORF, MARYLAND, INSTEAD OF PHILADELPHIA.

INVERTED JENNY STAMP.

DOUGLAS WORLD CRUISER

ALTHOUGH AMERICANS
HAD BEEN FIRST TO TAKE A CONTROLLED FLIGHT IN A HEAVIER-THAN-AIR VEHICLE, THEY QUICKLY LOST GROUND IN AVIATION TECHNOLOGY.

THE *CHICAGO* IN FLIGHT; LIEUTENANT LESLIE ARNOLD IS SEEN STANDING UP IN THE REAR COCKPIT.

By the 1920s countries in Europe had established commercial air travel and built many innovative airplanes.

In 1924 flying was still relatively new. The Jenny and other airplanes could not yet fly long distances. But airmen in six countries (the United States, Britain, France, Italy, Portugal, and Argentina) decided to try to circumnavigate the globe by flight. It became a race, because the winner would gain the prestige of being the first to fly around the world. The U.S. Army sent eight men in four airplanes in an attempt to win. The planes were Douglas World Cruisers, named for four U.S. cities: *Chicago, New Orleans, Seattle,* and *Boston.* They set out from Seattle on April 6, traveling west.

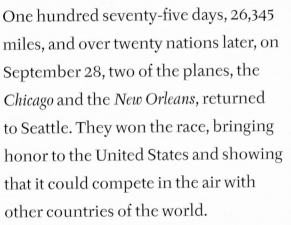

One hundred seventy-five days, 26,345 miles, and over twenty nations later, on September 28, two of the planes, the *Chicago* and the *New Orleans*, returned to Seattle. They won the race, bringing honor to the United States and showing that it could compete in the air with other countries of the world.

The four pilots and four mechanics surmounted many obstacles and endured much discomfort on their journey. The modified Douglas "torpedo bombers" had open cockpits, which didn't provide sufficient protection from the extreme weather they encountered. The planes had to be heavy enough to carry a lot of fuel, fast and nimble enough to face various emergencies, and rugged enough to survive rough oceans. Certain legs of the trip required wheels and others needed pontoons, so the change between the two had to be easy.

① WORLD FLIERS AT SAND POINT, WASHINGTON, AT BEGINNING OF FLIGHT (*LEFT TO RIGHT*): TURNER (DID NOT GO ON FLIGHT), OGDEN, ARNOLD, WADE, SMITH, MARTIN, HARVEY. NELSON AND HARDING ARE NOT PRESENT.

② THE *CHICAGO* BEING HOISTED BY CRANE IN HONG KONG.

Other challenges included a scarcity of landing fields, tricky navigation around icebergs and mountains, difficult weather such as fog, unfamiliar cultures, and the fragile airplanes themselves.

The Army identified eighteen supply and repair depots along the around-the-world route. It received support from the Navy, which transported fuel to remote locations. The Coast Guard also monitored the trip and provided accommodations for the fliers.

Less than a month into the trip, the *Seattle* crashed into a mountain in Alaska. It had separated from the three other crews, and for a time no one knew what had happened to it. Fortunately, its crew survived and found their way to a fish cannery in Port Moller on the coast.

On two separate occasions the remaining three aircraft encountered major mechanical problems. In present-day Vietnam, the *Chicago*'s engine overheated and the plane was suddenly forced to land on a remote lagoon. It needed a new engine. The other planes landed, gave the crew their supplies, and then continued on to the next planned stop. With some difficulty, a new engine was sent to the crew, who repaired the plane and resumed their journey. Then, months later, over the North Sea, the *Boston* had mechanical troubles and was forced to land on the open water. The Navy came to the rescue, but while the plane was being towed, the seas got rough and the airmen were forced to make the tough decision to cut the ropes and let the plane sink.

Ultimately, however, with two planes successfully finishing, the trip around the globe was a public relations triumph for the U.S. Army and the country in general. The flight generated excitement for flying and showed that the United States could compete on the aviation world stage.

ON THE GROUND, PROBABLY
IN BAGHDAD, IRAQ.

GODDARD ROCKET

★

AS A BOY IN
MASSACHUSETTS, ROBERT GODDARD
LOVED TO BE OUTDOORS AND TO LOOK
AT THE STARS.

He developed a fascination for flight, first for kites and then for balloons. He once tried to create a balloon out of aluminum and fill it with hydrogen, but it was too heavy to float. After reading H. G. Wells's *The War of the Worlds*, the seventeen-year-old Goddard had a vivid daydream. He was in a cherry tree in his parents' backyard, and he pictured himself ascending to Mars in a spinning spacecraft. He later identified this as the start of his lifelong obsession with finding a way to make space travel feasible.

In 1909, after years of investigation,

ROBERT GODDARD HOLDING ON TO THE LAUNCH STAND OF A LIQUID-FUEL ROCKET PRIOR TO ITS TEST LAUNCH ON MARCH 8, 1926, AT A FARM IN AUBURN, MASSACHUSETTS.

Goddard realized that a rocket was a workable propulsion system for spaceflight. A talented physics student, he quickly worked out the equations. Little did he know that at the same time several men in Europe were also puzzling through equations and discovering the rocket as the key to spaceflight. Goddard was one of three men (along with the Russian Konstantin Tsiolkovsky and the Romanian-German Hermann Oberth) who accomplished this. He published his research in early 1920 in a technical article in which he very briefly broached the idea that a rocket could escape gravity and reach the Moon.

Goddard's bold vision for spaceflight garnered much public attention. After his 1920 paper, newspapers around the nation were talking about Goddard: "New Rocket Devised by Prof. Goddard May Hit Face of the Moon" blared the *Boston Herald*. At first some scoffed at his ideas. A *New York Times* editorial titled "A Severe Strain on Credulity" wrongly accused Goddard of misunderstanding basic scientific principles. However, only a few years later the *Times* took him more seriously, with a detailed article under the headline "Hopes to Reach Moon with a Giant Rocket." And the newspaper retracted its editorial with a correction . . . in 1969, during the *Apollo 11* mission.

In March 1926, Goddard conducted his first launch with liquid-propellant rockets. The test, done on a relative's farm near Auburn, Massachusetts, reached a height of 41 feet and traveled 184 feet across the ground. For modern rocketry this launch is comparable to the Wright brothers' first flight.

Before Goddard invented his rocket, only gunpowder-based rockets like fireworks existed. Goddard was convinced

GODDARD WITH ROCKET FUELED BY LIQUID OXYGEN AND GASOLINE, WORCESTER, MASSACHUSETTS, 1926.

that he could build a new type of rocket capable of escaping Earth's gravity and going into space. It would require a fuel that could give a rocket greater speed than gunpowder-based fuel.

Goddard gained worldwide attention again in 1929, when a rocket of his crashed, attracting the local police and fire departments and the press. People began to complain about his rocket tests. The publicity about his work eventually caught the interest of the world-famous aviator Charles Lindbergh. With Lindbergh's help, Goddard moved his research lab from Massachusetts to Roswell, New Mexico. There he could conduct experiments in a more secluded but wide-open, tree-free environment. His rockets continued to fly higher and faster, and by the mid-1930s they had reached an altitude of almost two miles and had exceeded the speed of sound.

GODDARD WITH AN UNIDENTIFIED ROCKET UNDER CONSTRUCTION IN HIS WORKSHOP AT ROSWELL, NEW MEXICO, 1935.

Goddard ended up creating the world's first flying, liquid-fuel rocket. He proved that liquid-fuel rockets provide much greater thrust (power). No gunpowder-based rockets can achieve such velocities, although modern solid-fuel rockets, using other propellants, can.

Unfortunately, Goddard's desire for secrecy and his shortcomings as an engineer greatly limited his influence on later rocketry. Still, his work made an impact on the world's imagination. Although many before him had dreamed about the possibility of spaceflight, Goddard's calculations and experiments proved that a properly designed rocket could indeed escape Earth's gravity. Indeed, some people have called Robert Goddard the "Father of the Space Age."

SPIRIT OF ST. LOUIS

LESS THAN A HUNDRED
YEARS AGO, TRAVELERS CROSSING THE ATLANTIC OCEAN HAD ONLY ONE CHOICE: LARGE SHIPS CALLED OCEAN LINERS.

The vast distance of open water was a barrier, both psychologically and physically. Airplanes were still a new technology. Their engines were not powerful enough and their frames not sturdy enough to carry the heavy fuel load needed to travel long distances. The first successful flight across the Atlantic occurred in 1919. A U.S. Navy "flying boat" with a crew of six left from New York and hopped across the Atlantic following a northern route that ended in Portugal. Two weeks later two British aviators flew a nonstop route from Newfoundland to Ireland. Within eight years more than one hundred people had flown across the Atlantic—but no one had flown alone.

A New York hotel owner named Raymond Orteig wanted to encourage the progress of flight. He offered $25,000 to the first aviators to fly directly across the Atlantic Ocean between New York and Paris. He was sure it could be done.

Many pilots made the attempt, and some died trying. Finally, on May 20–21, 1927, Charles A. Lindbergh, a young airmail pilot and barnstormer, succeeded. He flew his Ryan NYP, named the *Spirit of St. Louis*, on the first *solo* nonstop flight across the Atlantic. He traveled from New York to Paris, a distance of about 3,610 miles (5,800 kilometers). He fought exhaustion for thirty-three and a half hours—after having been awake for the entire day *before* his takeoff from Roosevelt Field on Long Island,

New York. Fortunately, the *Spirit*, unstable because of its small fin and rudder, woke him several times as it started to spin out of control. Lindbergh's fatigue disappeared when he made landfall over Ireland and realized that he would reach his goal in a few more hours.

When he arrived over Paris, it was nighttime and he wasn't exactly sure where the airport was located. Then he noticed long lines of headlights leading to a brightly lit field. He had no idea that there was a crowd of 150,000 people waiting to greet him.

The instant he landed at Le Bourget Airport, Charles Lindbergh became an international celebrity. People around the world were amazed by his daring feat and called him "Lucky Lindy." By flying directly over the Atlantic Ocean from one large city to another, he demonstrated that vast distances were no longer barriers. After this, long-distance air travel would quickly become a reality.

Immense crowds welcomed him wherever he went: Europe, the United States, and Latin America.

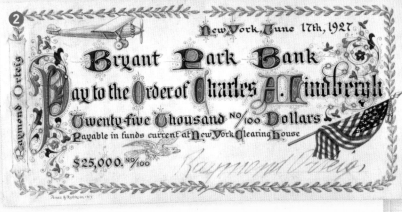

❶ LINDBERGH IN FRONT OF THE *SPIRIT OF ST. LOUIS*.

❷ THE ORTEIG PRIZE CHECK THAT CHARLES LINDBERGH RECEIVED FOR HIS TRANSATLANTIC FLIGHT.

COCKPIT OF THE *SPIRIT OF ST. LOUIS*, SHOWING THE FORWARD INSTRUMENT PANEL, STICK, THROTTLE, RUDDER PEDALS, AND FUEL CONTROL SYSTEM.

Fame engulfed him. Many other famous people wanted to meet him—including King George V of Britain. He had followed Lindbergh's flight with great interest and had one burning question for the aviator: He wanted to know how Lindbergh had urinated during his flight.

The fact that Lindbergh had survived the flight was astounding, but that he had chosen to fly in a single-engine plane was even more incredible. What if the engine had failed? In addition, to save weight and allow for more fuel, he hadn't carried a radio or a parachute.

Who was this unknown young man

LINDBERGH ARRIVES AT CROYDON AERODROME, NEAR LONDON, SHORTLY AFTER HIS TRANSATLANTIC FLIGHT.

with such confidence? Lindbergh once said, "What kind of man would live where there is no danger? I don't believe in taking foolish chances. But nothing can be accomplished by not taking a chance at all."

Born a year before the first airplane flew, Lindbergh grew up on a farm in Minnesota. He dropped out of college after two years because he wanted to fly. After a few years in the Army training to be an Army Air Service reserve pilot, he took a job flying the mail between Chicago and St. Louis. He was only twenty-five years old when he made his transatlantic flight and suddenly became one of the most famous people on the planet. And Lindbergh's triumphant flight drew the attention and adulation of his fellow Americans most of all.

Before Lindbergh's transatlantic flight, few people flew. His achievement revealed the huge potential of air travel. Public investment in aviation stocks soared as interest in the newly formed airlines increased, giving the industry a solid financial foundation. Lindbergh actively promoted the rapid growth of the U.S. airline industry. He continued to fly and, along with his wife, Anne, took several long-distance flights to survey possible commercial air routes. Lindbergh supported commercial aviation throughout his life. He was also friends with the rocket pioneer Robert Goddard, and he lived to see men walk on the Moon.

THE *SPIRIT OF ST. LOUIS* ON DISPLAY AT THE NATIONAL AIR AND SPACE MUSEUM. NOTICE THAT THERE IS NO FRONT WINDOW.

FULL SCALE WIND TUNNEL

A WIND TUNNEL—
A LARGE TUBE WITH AIR FLOWING THROUGH IT—IS A CRITICAL RESEARCH TOOL FOR DESIGNING EFFICIENT AIRCRAFT.

Wind tunnels give engineers important data about how aircraft will fly and help ensure a safe design. The Wright brothers pioneered the use of wind tunnels to test their airfoil and wing shapes for the design of the world's first successful airplane, the 1903 Wright Flyer.

One massive wind tunnel operated for more than seventy-eight years, and virtually every American fighter airplane was tested in it. Its fan, one of two in NASA's Full Scale Wind Tunnel in Hampton, Virginia, generated wind speeds of up to 120 miles per hour!

A TECHNICIAN CHECKS A WIND TUNNEL FAN MOTOR USED TO TEST A FULL-SIZE AIRCRAFT IN THE NASA FULL SCALE WIND TUNNEL.

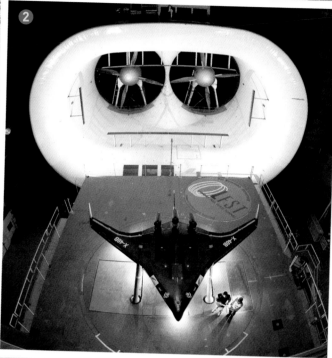

1 FULL SCALE WIND TUNNEL BUILDING, HAMPTON, VIRGINIA, WITH THE ENGINE HOUSE IN THE FOREGROUND.

2 INTERIOR SHOT SHOWING THE MASSIVE FAN BLADES.

Whereas smaller wind tunnels could test only models, this huge tunnel could test full-size planes. Also known as the 30-by-60-Foot Tunnel, it could hold an aircraft with a wingspan of up to 40 feet (12 meters)! It enabled aerospace engineers to see how the air flowed around the object, and the accurate data were used to test initial designs and make improvements.

The Full Scale Wind Tunnel was one of the most significant and versatile research tunnels ever built. It was a major factor in establishing the worldwide presence of the United States in aviation. The National Advisory Committee for Aeronautics (the NACA, predecessor to NASA) built it in 1931. It had its own power station to supply the energy needed for the two 4,000-horsepower motors that ran the huge propellers. For twelve years it was the largest wind tunnel in the world.

The NACA and then NASA have conducted research in aeronautics and astronautics since 1915. During the early twentieth century the study of aeronautics developed rapidly. Most of the NACA's aeronautical work took place at the Langley Memorial Aeronautical Laboratory (now the Langley Research Center) in Hampton, the site of the Full Scale Wind Tunnel and other historic wind tunnels. The research center was named after the third secretary of the Smithsonian, Samuel Pierpont Langley, an early aviation pioneer. Work there continues to this day.

The Full Scale Wind Tunnel provided data on many military and civil aviation designs, including full-scale aircraft, free-flight models of helicopters, lifting bodies, supersonic transports, and modern military aircraft. The XP-59A aircraft, the Mercury spacecraft, and the scale version of the X-15 aircraft—all described in this book—were tested in the Full Scale Wind Tunnel with this fan.

In one case the tunnel even tested enemy aircraft! On March 6, 1943, during World War II, a top-secret, two-day test took place in the Full Scale Wind Tunnel—the most secret test ever conducted in the facility. On June 4, 1942, Japanese warplanes had attacked the American military base at Dutch Harbor, Alaska. During the attack American guns hit a Japanese Mitsubishi Zero fighter airplane, and the pilot made an emergency landing. The airplane ended up in a bog covered with water and mud. Upon landing it had flipped over, and the pilot had died. A U.S. Navy patrol

WORKERS CRAFT THE WOODEN FAN BLADES.

spotted the crashed plane a month later. The military inspected it and realized it was a valuable prize: It was the first flyable Japanese Zero to fall into U.S. hands.

The military tested the airplane, first in San Diego and then in Washington, D.C. Next it was flown to the NACA's Langley Memorial Laboratory for the installation of special instruments. It arrived at Langley at about 3:00 P.M. on Friday, March 5, 1943. That night, under the cover of darkness, the Zero was mounted in the Full Scale Wind Tunnel, and for two days it was tested. A special wind tunnel crew was sworn to absolute secrecy. When light dawned on Monday morning, the airplane was back at its original location on the flight line, as if nothing had happened. The secret was only revealed sixty-seven years later, and no photographs of the Zero in the wind tunnel exist. Officials are even unsure where the test results ended up. But the tests demonstrated the value of the Full Scale Wind Tunnel: The military could study every inch of any airplane and learn its weaknesses and vulnerabilities, to the benefit of American pilots. Some pilots later credited the information they received in briefings about the Zero with saving their lives.

By the 1990s the tunnel was threatened with demolition due to the high cost of maintaining it. NASA worked out a plan allowing Old Dominion University, in Norfolk, Virginia, to operate the tunnel from 1996 until 2009. During this time many non-aviation vehicles were tested, including trucks, trains, automobiles, and even NASCAR race cars! The tunnel eventually was demolished, in 2010. The only artifact that remains from this historic tunnel is one of the two drive fans.

FAN BLADE IN THE NATIONAL AIR AND SPACE MUSEUM.

DOUGLAS DC-3

★

WITH THE INVENTION

OF THE AIRPLANE, PEOPLE QUICKLY
REALIZED THE POTENTIAL OF THIS NEW TYPE OF
TRANSPORTATION TO CHANGE THE WAY THEY TRAVELED.

Only ten years after the Wright Flyer lifted off the ground, the world's first scheduled airline began service. A man named Abram C. Pheil paid $400 in 1914 to become the first passenger on an airline. The airline was named the St. Petersburg–Tampa Airboat Line, and it flew across Tampa Bay in Florida. The flight covered 18 miles (29 kilometers) and took twenty-three minutes. This was eleven hours less than it took to travel between St. Petersburg and Tampa by train. However, after flying 1,204 passengers,

ABRAM C. PHEIL (*CENTER*), FORMER MAYOR OF ST. PETERSBURG, FLORIDA, AND THE FIRST PASSENGER ON THE ST. PETERSBURG-TAMPA AIRBOAT LINE.

DOUGLAS DC-3.

the airline shut down because it could not make enough money to stay in business.

The U.S. Post Office Department began building a network of airmail service routes. Once it had established a reliable airmail system, the department turned over airmail delivery to private airlines. The U.S. government continued to regulate the airways and encourage airline growth.

In Europe the Dutch airline, KLM, began operation in 1919. (It's the oldest carrier in the world still flying under its original name.) Longer-distance airlines in the United States began in 1926 and greatly expanded business in the 1930s. To begin with, they needed to convince potential passengers that flying was a better option than other modes of transportation.

The standard way to travel long distances was by railroad or ocean liner. Airplanes had propellers, which meant they traveled more slowly than they do now, but they

SURELY, SILENTLY, SWIFTLY

SKY CHIEF

OVERNIGHT—AND EVERY NIGHT—this Monarch of the Skies crosses America. Other TWA luxury Skyliners offer daylight flights between California, Chicago and New York in both directions. And every plane is equipped with three radio receiving sets and a transmitter, operating on four frequencies—two day and two night.

TWA is the only airline in the world completely equipped with Sperry Gyro-Pilots and Automatic Stabilizers which assure smooth, steady flight. The Gyro-Pilot allows the human pilot ample time for flight supervision and scientific navigation.

Directional radio beams provide a broad highway which guides the pilot safely and surely to his next scheduled stop. In addition TWA maintains the most complete weather forecasting service and meteorological staff of any U. S. airline.

It is no wonder more and more passengers are choosing TWA. If you, too, want the utmost in comfort and dependability, call any TWA office, Penna. R. R., or leading hotels and travel bureaus.

DOUGLAS SKYLINERS
On Every Flight

THE *Lindbergh* LINE

FASTEST
SHORTEST
...COAST
TO COAST

TRANSCONTINENTAL & WESTERN AIR, INC.

DC-3 FEATURED IN AN ADVERTISEMENT FOR THE TWA SKY CHIEF ROUTE.

still traveled faster than trains and ships. Through advertising, airlines were tempting people to try flying. Airlines also needed to convince potential passengers that flying was safe.

America's airline industry grew rapidly, from carrying only 6,000 passengers in 1929 to more than 450,000 in 1934 and 1.2 million in 1938. Still, only a small fraction of the traveling public flew. It was expensive! Only business executives and the wealthy could afford to fly. But the DC-3 (the initials stand for Douglas Commercial) helped to popularize air travel.

The shiny Douglas DC-3 first flew in 1935. It became the most successful airliner in the early years of commercial aviation and was the first to make a profit for airlines. It was also the first transport airplane that could fly passengers without a mail subsidy (the money the government paid for transporting mail by air) and still make a profit. Douglas produced more than 13,000 DC-3s, both civil and military. Many are still flying! The Douglas DC-3 transformed commercial air travel. Some people consider it the world's most famous commercial airplane. The DC-3 evolved from the DST, or Douglas Sleeper Transport. The DST featured sleeper berths (beds) and carried fourteen passengers for overnight flights. The DC-3 became the daytime version of this, with twenty-one seats. Passengers in the DC-3 could get from New York to Los Angeles in less than sixteen hours. And they could sleep in a berth on the way.

The DC-3's streamlined, versatile design and strong wing construction made it an exceptional aircraft. Today the plane is still in use around the world, more than eighty years after it first flew. Its many uses include fighting fires and transporting freight, passengers, military supplies, even skydivers. It can take off and land on grass or dirt runways, making it popular where there are no paved runways. As of summer 2015 one commercial airline, Buffalo Airways, far north in the Northwest Territories of Canada, still flies DC-3s and lands them on the snow-covered lakes. It is truly versatile, durable, and eternal!

TWO WOMEN CHAT OVER A MEAL ABOARD AN AMERICAN AIRLINES DOUGLAS SLEEPER TRANSPORT. MEALS WERE SERVED ON PORTABLE TABLES SET WITH CHINA, GLASSWARE, SILVERWARE, AND A VASE WITH FRESH FLOWERS.

UAVs

★

MANY PEOPLE
HAVE SEEN REMOTE-CONTROLLED MODEL AIRPLANES FLYING AT THE PARK OR THE BEACH. THEY ARE A TYPE OF DRONE.

Officially called a UAV (for unmanned, or unpiloted, aerial vehicle), a drone refers to a robotic aircraft that the pilot flies from a distance. Drones come in all shapes and sizes and are used for many activities. The military has used drones in some form or other going all the way back to World War I. Today drones are increasingly used for civilian activities, such as aerial surveys of crops and livestock, search-and-rescue operations, crowd monitoring, forest fire detection, border patrol missions, police surveillance, weather research (flying into hurricanes), and delivery of supplies to remote disaster areas. Drones even filmed skiing and snowboarding events during the 2014 Winter Olympics in Sochi, Russia.

Drones are increasingly popular today. But they've been around a long time. One, named the OQ-2 Radioplane, was the first mass-produced UAV in the United States. It has an interesting story. An English movie actor named Reginald Denny lived in Hollywood in the 1930s. He had served in the Royal Flying Corps during World War I and liked airplanes. Like many actors in the 1920s, he took up flying for fun. He became interested in radio-controlled model airplanes and opened a hobby shop on Hollywood Boulevard that sold model airplanes, trains, and ships. People around the country could order his models by mail, including his signature "Dennyplane."

In the late 1930s he met an American general who complained how expensive it was for the Army to use airplanes to tow targets for shooting practice. Denny and his business partner, Nelson Paul Whittier, suggested radio-controlled planes and demonstrated one to the Army. Even though the radio failed and the model crashed, the Army agreed to buy three planes. Denny and Whittier refined their models and made a series of improvements. The Army ordered fifty more of them. Eventually the OQ-2 Radioplane was complete. Denny's company, Radioplane, ended up manufacturing thousands of these drones

REGINALD DENNY WITH MODEL PLANE.

for the Army during World War II. They were used to teach soldiers how to precisely hit targets in the air. After the war Radioplane was purchased by Northrop, one of the leading American aircraft manufacturers.

One young woman named Norma Jeane Dougherty worked in Denny's Radioplane factory, spraying airplane parts with fire retardant and inspecting parachutes. A U.S. Army photographer on assignment to document women helping with the war effort visited the factory. He took photos of Norma Jeane and, captivated by her good looks, encouraged her to apply to a modeling agency. She did, bleached her hair blond, and changed her name. She eventually became one of America's most famous movie stars: Marilyn Monroe. The photographer's commanding officer

NORMA JEANE DOUGHERTY—LATER
CALLED MARILYN MONROE—AT WORK IN
THE RADIOPLANE FACTORY, 1945.

DRAGANFLYER DRONE.

who suggested he visit Denny's factory just happened to be the future U.S. president
Ronald Reagan.

Today police departments are also using drones. In 2013 a man in Canada crashed
his car in a remote area. Injured and disoriented, he wandered away from the crash
site and was in danger of freezing to death. Police used a Draganflyer drone equipped
with an infrared camera to find the man. Considered the first drone used to save a
human life, it is now part of the National Air and Space Museum's collection.

Recent advances in UAV technology have transformed the way we interact. Drone
technology allows the military to go into enemy areas, conducting surveillance and
collecting information, and to engage in combat with enemy forces without putting
the controllers in danger. UAV technology will continue to change military strategies
and procedures. New types of drones will also allow civilians to accomplish their jobs
in creative ways.

BELL XP-59A AIRACOMET; WHITTLE AND JUMO 004B ENGINES

★

A CENTURY AGO
IT TOOK A WEEK TO CROSS THE AMERICAN CONTINENT BY TRAIN.

The DC-3, which used propellers, took about fifteen hours, with three refueling stops. Today it takes less than six hours by jet airliner. The story of the jet engine begins during World War II.

In 1941, European countries were already at war. American military leaders recognized that the United States lagged behind in airplane technology, so General Henry H. "Hap" Arnold of the U.S. Army Air Corps (just before it became the Army Air Forces) formed a special group to investigate new technologies in Europe. He watched the flight of a new British airplane (the British Gloster E.28/39) that was powered by a new type of engine, a turbojet. Impressed, he acquired sample engines and production rights and decided to try to develop a jet aircraft in the United States. The military selected a company named Bell Aircraft to do the job.

Bell soon unveiled the XP-59A Airacomet. It was America's first step into the jet age. Test pilot Robert M. Stanley was the first to fly an Airacomet, on October 1, 1942. But the United States didn't want the world to know about its jet, so the project was originally top secret.

THE BELL XP-59A IN FLIGHT.

THE BELL XP-59A IN FLIGHT.

THE XP-59A AT MUROC DRY LAKE IN CALIFORNIA. NOTICE THE DUMMY PROPELLER ON THE NOSE, MEANT TO DISGUISE THE AIRACOMET AS A CONVENTIONAL AIRCRAFT.

ANN BAUMGARTNER, THE FIRST AMERICAN WOMAN TO FLY A JET-POWERED AIRCRAFT.

To maintain secrecy during its initial tests at Muroc Dry Lake in California, Bell mounted a dummy propeller on the nose to disguise the Airacomet as a conventional aircraft. Mechanics removed it before flight and reinstalled it afterward.

Bell was known for innovative design. But for the Airacomet, its engineers developed a conventional-style airplane that incorporated the new type of engine. The large, thick, midwing design promoted stable handling. Although designed as a fighter, the Airacomet proved to be underpowered during its test program and flew more slowly than the normal piston-engine fighters. The XP-59A did not see combat.

Ann G. Baumgartner (later Carl) was one of the pilots who got to fly this new airplane. When Baumgartner was young, her father had taken her to watch airmail pilots landing at the airport in Newark, New Jersey. She was inspired to become a pilot when the aviatrix Amelia Earhart visited her elementary school class. Baumgartner would become the first American woman to fly a jet-powered aircraft.

A member of the Women Airforce Service Pilots (WASP) program, Baumgartner flew an XP-59A on October 14, 1944. She is considered a jet age pioneer and was the only American woman to test-fly experimental planes during World War II. She later became a science journalist and wrote *A WASP Among Eagles*, a book about her experiences as a test pilot during the war. Some 25,000 women applied for the WASP program, but only 1,800 were selected and just 1,000 received their wings. Thirty-eight of the women lost their lives while in service.

The XP-59A served as an advanced trainer and gave the Army Air Forces and the Navy valuable experience with jet aircraft technology. It is the original ancestor of generations of American military and civil jet aircraft. The P-59 and other early jet aircraft demonstrated the power and efficiency of this new type of engine. These advances produced a new generation of airliners— jetliners—making air travel fast and affordable.

THIS ARMY AIR FORCES RECRUITMENT POSTER ENVISIONED THE P-59 AS THE FUTURE OF COMBAT AIRCRAFT.

WHITTLE AND JUMO 004 ENGINES

In the past, airplanes used propellers, which spin fast to generate the thrust needed to fly through the air. Propeller aircraft are noisy and generate vibrations. A jet engine allows an airplane to travel much faster by drawing in large quantities of air. The high-pressure air is then ignited and propelled at high speed out the back of the engine. The jet makes a loud whooshing noise, but the flight is usually smooth.

Two people, Sir Frank Whittle of Britain and Dr. Hans Pabst von Ohain of Germany, were developing a jet engine at the same time but didn't know about each other's work.

SIR FRANK WHITTLE (*LEFT*) CHATS WITH HANS PABST VON OHAIN IN WASHINGTON, D.C., OCTOBER 24, 1974.

Whittle began developing his engine in 1930 while serving with the Royal Air Force. The RAF considered the concept impracticable, so Whittle turned to private financial support. He founded his own company and successfully tested a prototype in April 1937. Although the undeveloped jet engine demonstrated great potential, the British Air Ministry chose to concentrate its limited financial resources on other projects.

Finally, in 1939, the Air Ministry placed an order with Whittle for a turbojet to power its new Gloster E.28/39 test aircraft. As development of the engine progressed, the Gloster made a few short, straight hops into the air in April 1941, which marked the first unofficial flight of a British jet aircraft. The first official flight occurred a month later.

Meanwhile, in Germany, von Ohain began developing a turbojet engine in the 1930s while studying at the University of Göttingen. On August 27, 1939, his jet engine became the first to fly, in a Heinkel He 178 airplane.

Soon Germany was producing on a large scale a much-improved design by Anselm Franz. The first axial-flow Junkers Jumo 004 turbojets came off the production line in mid-1943; Germany built nearly 6,000 Jumo 004 engines by the end of World War II.

The Jumo 004 engine is just one of many German technical advances developed during World War II. But by the time the engine was available in significant numbers, the Allied forces fighting against Germany were winning the war. It had no effect on the war's outcome.

JUNKERS JUMO 004
TURBOJET ENGINE.

BELL X-1, GLAMOROUS GLENNIS

IN 1947 NO ONE
REALLY KNEW IF IT WAS POSSIBLE TO FLY FASTER THAN THE SPEED OF SOUND (CALLED "MACH 1").

Most scientists thought that shock waves would break up an airplane at that speed. People imagined an invisible wall called the "sound barrier." They thought that this wall would destroy airplanes.

Test pilots like to take calculated risks and live on the edge. British test pilot Geoffrey de Havilland Jr. tried to break through the sound barrier, but he was killed in 1946 when his airplane, the "Swallow," disintegrated on one of his attempts. This discouraged the British from trying any further test flights.

Instead, a bright orange American airplane named *Glamorous Glennis* became the first plane to fly faster than sound. Piloted by Captain Charles E. "Chuck" Yeager of the U.S. Air Force, the Bell X-1 (X for "experimental") reached 700 miles (1,127 kilometers) per hour—Mach 1.06—on October 14, 1947. The aircraft was originally called the XS-1 for "experimental-supersonic." Yeager named it *Glamorous Glennis* after his wife.

How did it work? To overcome dangerous aerodynamic forces, the X-1 had extremely thin yet strong wings and a minutely adjustable horizontal stabilizer on the tail to improve control. Designers shaped the fuselage like a .50-caliber bullet, because high-powered bullets were stable at supersonic speeds. The X-1 was dropped from the bomb bay of a Boeing B-29 Superfortress at 23,000 feet (7,000 meters) and used its rocket engine to climb to its test altitude.

Yeager was the Air Force's most experienced test pilot. A World War II ace with eleven victories, the West Virginia native loved speed. He was known as a skilled pilot with an innate understanding of machines. And he could stay cool under pressure. Major General Fred J. Ascani said that Yeager was "the only pilot I've ever flown with who gives the impression that he's part of the cockpit hardware, so in tune with the machine that instead of being flesh and blood, he could be an autopilot."

Before his scheduled flight, Yeager broke two ribs. Afraid of being removed from the mission, he told only his wife and Jack Ridley, the X-1 project engineer. With his injury, Yeager was unable to seal the hatch of the X-1 by himself, so Ridley suggested that he use the end of a broom handle as a lever to close the hatch on the day of the flight. A broom helped Yeager make history!

Only three X-1s were ever built. The *Glamorous Glennis* flew seventy-eight times—as fast as Mach 1.45 and as high as 71,900 feet (21,900 meters). The X-1 program gathered crucial flight data about transonic and supersonic flight for the Air Force and the National Advisory Committee for Aeronautics (NACA), NASA's predecessor. It was the first of a series of experimental piloted and unpiloted projects, identified beginning with an X, that continues to this day.

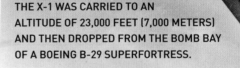

THE BELL X-1 ON DISPLAY AT THE NATIONAL AIR AND SPACE MUSEUM.

THE X-1 WAS CARRIED TO AN ALTITUDE OF 23,000 FEET (7,000 METERS) AND THEN DROPPED FROM THE BOMB BAY OF A BOEING B-29 SUPERFORTRESS.

CAPTAIN CHARLES E. "CHUCK" YEAGER POSES IN THE COCKPIT OF THE BELL X-1, WHICH HE NAMED *GLAMOROUS GLENNIS*, AT MUROC AIR FORCE BASE, CALIFORNIA, MAY 1948.

The X-1 experiments solved the challenge of transonic and supersonic flight but did not create the transformation people expected. Flying faster than sound proved too expensive for all but military applications, so the age of civil supersonic transport was brief. Nevertheless, the data gathered on transonic and supersonic flight has made new generations of civil subsonic airliners safer and more efficient.

At any rate, Chuck Yeager could say he was the first person to fly faster than sound. After his first flight he said, "I realized that the mission had to end in a letdown because the real barrier wasn't in the sky but in our knowledge and experience of supersonic flight." In other words, there wasn't really a sound barrier or wall after all.

YEAGER IN FRONT OF THE X-1 ON THE MORNING OF HIS HISTORIC FLIGHT.

BOEING 367-80, "DASH 80"

THE MILITARY
ADOPTED JET TECHNOLOGY FIRST, BUT COMMERCIAL AVIATION BEGAN TO CONSIDER IT SOON AFTER.

The Douglas Aircraft Company was successfully selling propeller airplanes to the airlines. But the Boeing Company decided to build a jet airplane to convince the airlines that jet technology was the future. The president of Boeing, Bill Allen, had witnessed the flight of the world's first jet airliner, the de Havilland Comet, at an air show in England. Boeing engineers developed the company's prototype jet plane, the 367-80 (called the "Dash 80" within Boeing), in secrecy. Its first flight took place in July 1954.

The following year Allen thought the airplane was ready for its official public debut. He invited airline company executives from across the United States and around the world to Seattle to attend the annual Seafair

ROLLOUT OF THE 367-80 AT THE BOEING PLANT, RENTON, WASHINGTON, MAY 14, 1954.

festival and hydroplane races. This was the perfect opportunity to impress them with a standard flyover of the 367-80. Test pilot Alvin "Tex" Johnston had his own ideas. The roar of the jet engines caught the crowd's attention. Then Johnston performed two barrel rolls in front of the stunned crowd: The airplane turned upside down and then right side up twice, as if rolling inside an invisible barrel that was on its side. Allen was dumbfounded. He called Johnston to his office the next day and asked the pilot what he had been doing. Johnston replied that he was just selling airplanes.

After its impressive debut, which was caught on film, the Dash 80 went into production as the Boeing 707 series. As the first commercially successful jet plane, it was popular for several decades. The 367-80 is given credit for ushering in the jet age, an era of faster and smoother air travel.

The 367-80 was later turned into an experimental plane that tested new technologies. Finally, Boeing staff retired it in 1969 and placed it into storage. Three years later Boeing donated it to the Smithsonian.

PAN AMERICAN WORLD AIRWAYS ORDER FOR JETS— THE LARGEST AIRCRAFT ORDER EVER BY AN AIRLINE UP TO THAT TIME—MADE HEADLINES IN 1955.

THE BOEING 367-80 WENT INTO PRODUCTION AS THE POPULAR BOEING 707.

SPUTNIK 1 AND EXPLORER 1

IN 1957 A SHINY
SILVER BALL THE SIZE OF A BASKETBALL
CAUGHT THE WORLD'S ATTENTION . . .
AND STARTED A SPACE RACE

between the United States and the Soviet Union (formed from present-day Russia and fourteen other countries). Both nations had declared their intentions to launch satellites for the International Geophysical Year, an eighteen-month worldwide science initiative that ended December 1958.

On October 4, 1957, the Soviet Union sent Sputnik 1, the world's first human-made satellite, into orbit around Earth. Sputnik contained a radio transmitter that sent back a distinctive "beep-beep-beep" signal on frequencies that could be received by radio operators around the world. Although the signal was weak, the message it sent was strong: The Soviet Union had initiated the Space Age. Sputnik's sphere was polished until shiny, to aid in tracking by telescope and to enhance its appearance. "This ball will be exhibited in museums!" proclaimed Sergei P. Korolev, the Soviet chief designer.

The launch of Sputnik scared many Americans and alarmed the country's leaders. It demonstrated that the Soviet Union could achieve something that the United

SPUTNIK 1 REPLICA ON DISPLAY AT THE NATIONAL AIR AND SPACE MUSEUM. LENT BY THE RUSSIAN FEDERATION. DESPITE SPUTNIK'S STREAMLINED APPEARANCE, IT WOBBLED WHILE IN ORBIT.

States could not. People could look up into the sky and with their own eyes see Sputnik traveling among the stars. They could turn their radios on and hear its beeping. As a result, Congress established the National Aeronautics and Space Administration (NASA) to promote space exploration and directed millions of dollars to go toward science and math education. But Sputnik also became a cultural sensation, inspiring interior design, popular music, and even jokes. The swing artist Louis Prima recorded "Beep! Beep!" in 1957. The historian Daniel J. Boorstin quipped, "Never before had so small and so harmless an object created such consternation."

Soviet premier Nikita Khrushchev liked Sputnik 1 so much that he ordered Korolev to launch a second satellite for the fortieth anniversary of the Bolshevik Revolution. On November 3, 1957, the larger and heavier Sputnik 2 carried a dog named Laika into orbit, heightening the sense of urgency in the United States. The Soviets had demonstrated their technological expertise yet again. What about the United States?

THIS RARE PHOTO OF SERGEI P. KOROLEV, THE SOVIET CHIEF DESIGNER, SHOWS HIM WITH ONE OF THE POSSIBLE SPACEFARING DOGS.

A month later the first American satellite launch effort failed spectacularly when its Vanguard rocket exploded during liftoff. The United States was embarrassed. However, on January 31, 1958, Explorer 1 was launched aboard an Army missile and became the first successful U.S. satellite. It contained a cosmic ray detector, a radio transmitter, and temperature and micrometeoroid sensors. Its flight marked America's entry in the space race—a new Cold War competition.

Space became a battlefield of the Cold War. It was not a physical war, although it did feature weapons, but more a war of ideas. Space was an unexplored region and an opportunity for competing countries to show off their technological prowess.

Besides showing the world that the United States could compete with the technological exploits of the Soviets, Explorer 1 made a major discovery: It detected intense radiation belts around Earth, doughnut-shaped zones of highly charged particles in the magnetic field of the planet. The Van Allen belts, as they are known, were named for Dr. James A. Van Allen, a physicist at the University of Iowa. It was Van Allen who directed the design and creation of Explorer's instruments. The Van Allen radiation belts protect life on Earth from cosmic radiation. They were the first major scientific discovery of the Space Age and remain a subject of research today.

Before Sputnik flew, there was nothing known orbiting Earth other than the Moon. Now thousands of active and inactive satellites ring the planet.

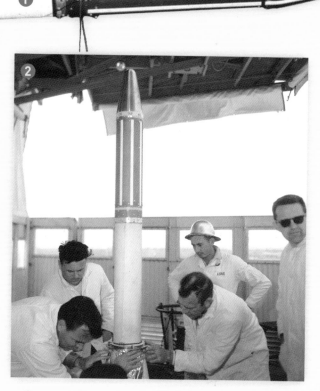

❶ EXPLORER 1 BACKUP, ON DISPLAY AT THE NATIONAL AIR AND SPACE MUSEUM. THE STRIPED FRONT SECTION OF EXPLORER CONTAINED THE PAYLOAD; THE REAR SECTION WAS A SOLID-FUEL ROCKET MOTOR. EXPLORER'S LIGHT AND DARK STRIPES HELPED CONTROL ITS TEMPERATURE. EXPLORER SPUN AROUND ITS LONG AXIS, EXTENDING FOUR FLEXIBLE ANTENNAS.

❷ TECHNICIANS PREPARE THE SATELLITE PRIOR TO LAUNCH.

❸ THREE KEY EXPLORER 1 TEAM MEMBERS TRIUMPHANTLY DISPLAY A FULL-SCALE MODEL OF THE SATELLITE AFTER ITS SUCCESSFUL LAUNCH (*LEFT TO RIGHT*): WILLIAM PICKERING, DIRECTOR OF THE JET PROPULSION LABORATORY, PASADENA, CALIFORNIA; JAMES A. VAN ALLEN, EXPLORER'S INSTRUMENT DESIGNER; AND WERNHER VON BRAUN, WHO DESIGNED THE JUPITER-C ROCKET THAT HELPED LAUNCH EXPLORER.

NORTH AMERICAN X-15

THE BELL X-1
WAS FAST, BUT THE NORTH AMERICAN X-15
WAS FASTER. MORE IMPORTANT, IT WAS ONE OF
THE WORLD'S FIRST OPERATIONAL SPACEPLANES.

THE ROCKET-POWERED X-15 WAS DROP-LAUNCHED—
RELEASED FROM UNDER THE WING OF A BOEING B-52
BOMBER AT AN ALTITUDE OF 40,000 FEET (12,000 METERS).

It bridged the gap between human flight within Earth's atmosphere and flight into space. Although X-15s stopped flying in 1968, nine years after their first flight, they still hold the official record for the world's fastest and highest-flying aircraft! These rocket-powered research aircraft explored the hypersonic region: speeds greater than Mach 5—five times the speed of sound! They became the first aircraft to reach speeds of Mach 4, Mach 5, and even beyond Mach 6 (4,567 miles per hour).

On thirteen of their flights, they entered what is classified as "space," qualifying the eight pilots for astronaut wings. (According to the U.S. Air Force, "space" begins 50 miles [80 kilometers] above Earth. The international definition, set by the Fédération Aéronautique Internationale, sets space as beginning 62.1 miles [100 kilometers] above Earth.)

The Smithsonian's X-15 is the first of three that were built. Only one other still exists. Although it did not set all of the records, this X-15 flew Mach 6 during the course of its eighty-two missions.

How did it work? Similar to the Bell X-1, it was "drop-launched." The rocket-powered X-15 was carried under the wing of a Boeing B-52 bomber to an altitude of 40,000 feet (12,000 meters) and then released.

The U.S. Air Force's X-15 program demonstrated the importance of research aircraft to flight technology. Its 199 flights gathered valuable data for the Mercury, Gemini, Apollo, and Space Shuttle programs. The X-15 pioneered new heat-resistant materials, as well as flight control systems that could transition between air and space.

A special high-strength nickel alloy known as Inconel X gave the X-15 its distinctive black color. Inconel X was highly resistant to heat while maintaining its strength. The X-15 could withstand temperatures of 1,200 degrees Fahrenheit.

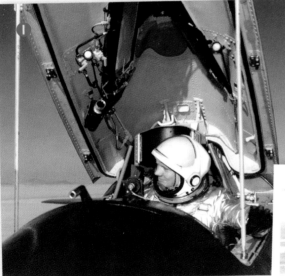

Among the twelve people who piloted the X-15s were the future *Apollo 11* commander and first person to step on the Moon, Neil Armstrong, and Space Shuttle astronaut Joe Engle. Armstrong called it "the most successful research airplane in history."

1 NEIL ARMSTRONG IN THE COCKPIT OF AN X-15, 1961.

2 SIX TEST PILOTS IN THEIR PRESSURE SUITS IN FRONT OF A NORTH AMERICAN X-15 (*LEFT TO RIGHT*): JOE ENGLE (U.S. AIR FORCE), ROBERT RUSHWORTH (USAF), JOHN MCKAY (NASA), WILLIAM "PETE" KNIGHT (USAF), MILTON THOMPSON (NASA), AND WILLIAM DANA (NASA).

TEST PILOT A. SCOTT CROSSFIELD IN FRONT OF THE FIRST X-15 AT THE NORTH AMERICAN PLANT, LOS ANGELES, OCTOBER 1958.

A. Scott Crossfield was the first pilot to fly the X-15. He also played a major role in its design and development. It was his responsibility to test the plane's airworthiness at high speeds, a very dangerous job. He made fourteen flights in the X-15—and had two close calls: when one of the plane's engines exploded shortly after launch and when a malfunctioning valve caused an explosion while he was seated in the plane on the ground. As a pilot, he enjoyed flying all kinds of different planes. Crossfield was honored by President John F. Kennedy twice for his contributions in advancing aeronautical science. Although he was known as a test pilot, Crossfield once said, "I am an aeronautical engineer, an aerodynamicist and a designer. My flying was only primarily because I felt that it was essential to designing and building better airplanes for pilots to fly." While he was in college, he worked at the University of Washington's wind tunnel. He earned a master of science degree in aeronautical engineering and was in the first generation of academically trained engineer–test pilots.

The X-15 served as a bridge between aviation and spaceflight by putting some of the first Americans into space. It was a predecessor to the Space Shuttle orbiter and other winged space vehicles.

DISCOVERER/CORONA

THE DISCOVERER/
CORONA SATELLITE HAD TWO NAMES, ONE PUBLIC AND ONE SECRET.

As the first U.S. "spy in the sky," it orbited more than ninety miles above Earth and took detailed photographs of people and objects. "Discoverer" was the cover (or public) name used in the early years of this highly classified program. Government officials told the public that the capsule was part of a Discoverer series, intended to gather scientific data and test the feasibility of recovering instrument packages from orbit. "Corona" was the top-secret name of this photoreconnaissance satellite

❶ FAIRCHILD C-119J FLYING BOXCAR IN FLIGHT OVER THE PACIFIC OCEAN, ABOUT TO MAKE A MIDAIR PICKUP OF THE DISCOVERER XXVI SATELLITE CAPSULE, DESCENDING ON A CHECKERED PARACHUTE, 1961.

❷ PRESIDENT DWIGHT D. EISENHOWER INSPECTS A RECOVERED DISCOVERER CAPSULE AT A CEREMONY IN THE WHITE HOUSE IN 1960.

program—using a camera to gather detailed information about an area—run by the U.S. Air Force and the Central Intelligence Agency.

The Discoverer XIII capsule was the first human-made object recovered from orbit. The U.S. Navy retrieved it from the Pacific Ocean, north of Hawaii, on August 11, 1960, after a day in orbit.

Although Discoverer XIII contained only instruments to record data about its flight, later Discoverer satellites carried cameras and film. The Soviet satellite Sputnik had established the precedent of satellites flying over other nations without their permission, and the Corona program was developed to collect data on the Soviet Union. A satellite in space was much less obvious than, for example, the U-2 spy planes that conducted missions over that country.

The program started out slowly, with many technical challenges, but after twelve failures it made a successful test flight. Engineers quickly figured out how to solve the problems, and by the mid-1960s the program was delivering a steady stream of valuable information.

The Corona program provided critical information to U.S. policymakers through the 1960s that helped maintain the Cold War balance of power. Only a small number of government officials knew of its existence and had access to the photographs and information it collected; the public did not learn about it until President Bill Clinton unveiled its existence in 1995. Although it cost many hundreds of millions of dollars, President Lyndon Johnson valued photoreconnaissance highly. "We've spent $35 or $40 billion on the space program. And if nothing else had come out of it except the knowledge that we gained from space photography, it would be worth ten times what the whole program has cost." By the end of the Corona program in 1972, 145 Corona satellites had successfully flown over and photographed the Soviet Union, China, and other nations.

How did it work? Corona used film, which had to be returned to Earth and developed in a laboratory. Launched on modified missiles, the satellites carried cameras, film, and a film-return capsule. Upon receiving commands from Earth, the cameras would begin exposing the film. When all the exposed film had been wound onto the reel in the return capsule, the capsule separated from the satellite and reentered Earth's atmosphere. At about 60,000 feet a parachute deployed, and the capsule was then snagged in midair by an Air Force C-119 plane in a recovery area northeast of Hawaii. A trapeze-like apparatus behind the aircraft had several hooks to snag the capsule's parachute lines. (If the retrieval plane did not catch the film capsule during descent, it fell into the ocean. A plug at its bottom disintegrated after a certain period, thus causing the capsule and its classified film to sink, which kept it from falling into the wrong hands.)

When a capsule was retrieved, the film was removed in Hawaii, developed in New York, and taken to Washington, D.C., for analysis. Modern satellites provide information much faster, of course. They transmit images electronically, which allows the satellites to remain in orbit longer and acquire more imagery.

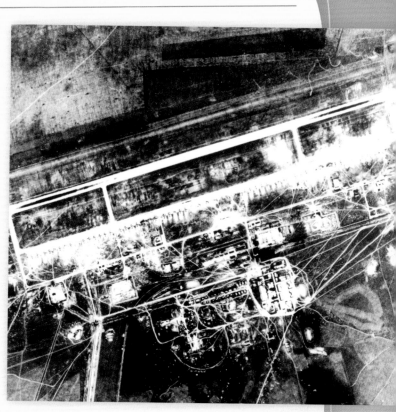

A 1966 CORONA IMAGE OF THE DOLON AIRFIELD IN THE SOVIET UNION, MAGNIFIED MORE THAN 20 TIMES.

ILLUSTRATION DEPICTING THE RECOVERY OF A DISCOVERER SATELLITE PAYLOAD, CIRCA 1960. A NAVY SHIP AND HELICOPTER ARE MAKING THEIR WAY TO THE EJECTED PAYLOAD.

The gold-plated reentry capsule and parachute were the only items recovered from the satellite. The rest of it quickly reentered the atmosphere and burned up. The upper stage, which maneuvered the capsule, was released in space. The capsule's heat shield was released when the parachute deployed.

One of the biggest challenges was cloudy weather in the target areas. The cameras could not see through cloud cover, so early efforts sometimes resulted in photos of clouds. Timely and accurate weather data was required. As a result, the government developed its classified weather satellite system, which solved the problem.

Discoverer XIII began an era of satellite observation of Earth from space for national security. Now we rely on satellite images not only for national security but also for weather prediction, climate monitoring, practical navigation, agricultural planning, and many other functions.

AN ENTIRE BUCKET
WITH FILM SPOOL.

TELSTAR

★

PEOPLE WHO

WATCH THE OLYMPICS OR OTHER
EVENTS THAT ARE BROADCAST LIVE FROM
FARAWAY PLACES CAN THANK TELSTAR.

Telstar 1, the first active communications satellite, began the era of live international television.

After its launch on July 10, 1962, it relayed television images between the United States and France and Britain. The grainy images of a taped performance by the French singer Yves Montand, a Philadelphia Phillies–Chicago Cubs baseball game, and a live news conference held by President John F. Kennedy were the first messages exchanged across the Atlantic Ocean among the citizens of the new "global village."

THE FLIGHT SPARE OF TELSTAR IN THE COLLECTION
OF THE NATIONAL AIR AND SPACE MUSEUM.

As someone at the Columbia Broadcasting System (CBS) later noted of the first broadcast: "It was only eight minutes long ... had no stars, no script ... [but] it was one of the most important television broadcasts ever presented."

Telstar, a contraction of the words "telecommunications" and "star," was a political as well as technical triumph for the United States in the space race. By 1962 the Soviet Union had scored a number of space firsts. It was technically capable of developing a communications satellite that could relay television images to the world. But the fact that the United States and its allies achieved it first made a statement. Telstar stood as a powerful symbol of the West's commitment to open societies and the freedom to communicate far and wide.

Orbiting around Earth, Telstar received signals from one Earth station and retransmitted them to another on a different continent. Since the spherical Telstar spun for stability, it was covered with small solar cells to ensure that it would always catch solar energy. The array of small microwave antenna horns around its middle guaranteed that one would always be pointing toward a station on Earth.

A BELL SYSTEM TECHNICIAN WORKS ON TELSTAR'S WIRING.

Telstar used ground stations in Maine in the United States, Pleumeur-Bodou in France, and Goonhilly Downs in England. A huge horn antenna in Andover, Maine, tracked and communicated with Telstar as it passed overhead. Because of the satellite's highly elliptical and relatively low orbit, it could relay communications for only twenty to thirty minutes at a time.

THE SCIENCE FICTION WRITER ARTHUR C. CLARKE STANDS ON THE SET OF THE FILM *2001: A SPACE ODYSSEY* (1968).

One person who foresaw this technology was Sir Arthur C. Clarke. He was a well-known author of nearly a hundred books on science fiction and science fact. A lifelong proponent of human space travel, he also cowrote the screenplay for the movie *2001: A Space Odyssey*, considered by many to be one of the most influential movies of all time because of its stunning special effects and provocative ideas about human evolution and other matters. Clarke loved to imagine life in the future, and he often took familiar devices and altered them into tools of the future. In 1945 he published a brief essay suggesting the use of space-based communications satellites to allow for more direct connections between continents. Clarke predicted "a rapid development of world-wide TV, so that major events in any part of the planet can be witnessed, live, over the whole globe." He foresaw a world of global connections in trade and cultural exchange, where communications satellites meant that distance didn't matter.

Beginning in 1963, communications satellites shifted to a geostationary orbit. At an altitude of 22,300 miles (35,880 kilometers), a satellite will appear to stay in place, as its orbital period matches the twenty-four-hour rotation of Earth. This greatly simplifies tracking.

Telstar I operated for only a few months. But it inaugurated an age of instant, worldwide television and media coverage, now a multibillion-dollar industry. The ability to watch live news, sports, and entertainment has made the world seem smaller.

MERCURY FRIENDSHIP 7

SOON AFTER

SPUTNIK SURPRISED THE AMERICANS, NASA DEVELOPED PROJECT MERCURY, A PROGRAM DESIGNED TO PUT AN AMERICAN INTO ORBIT.

NASA selected seven astronauts from a pool of test pilots. As America's first astronauts, the Mercury Seven became instant national celebrities. But before NASA would send a human into space, it sent a chimpanzee named Ham. Steered by an automatic control system, the capsule did not require a human pilot, and Ham returned safely. On May 5, 1961, Alan Shepard became the first American launched into space, with a fifteen-minute-long suborbital flight that took him to an altitude of 116 miles (187 kilometers). However, about three weeks earlier, on April 12, the Soviet space program had accomplished yet another big feat: Their cosmonaut (what the Soviets called an astronaut) Yuri Gagarin had blasted into space and had orbited Earth. He was the first man in space.

MERCURY *FRIENDSHIP 7* CAPSULE ON DISPLAY AT THE NATIONAL AIR AND SPACE MUSEUM.

Before sending an astronaut into orbit around Earth, NASA ran a "dress rehearsal" flight with the second chimpanzee in space, Enos. Almost three months later NASA astronaut John Glenn sat atop an Atlas rocket in a capsule not much larger than a refrigerator. A ball of flame erupted, launching the rocket into the Florida sky. Higher and higher he traveled, the details of Earth fading in the distance. On February 20, 1962, he became the first American to orbit Earth, in a spacecraft he named *Friendship 7*. In just

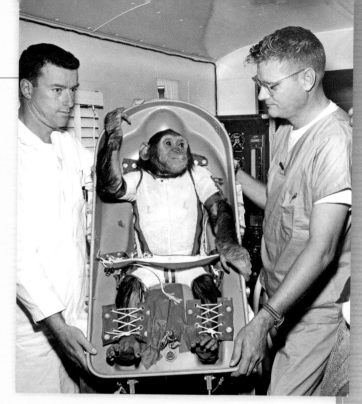

ONE OF THE CHIMPANZEES (PROBABLY HAM) ON THE COUCH IN WHICH HE RODE DURING HIS FLIGHT; WITH MEMBERS OF THE AEROMEDICAL FIELD LABORATORY, HOLLOMAN AIR FORCE BASE, NEW MEXICO.

under five hours, Glenn traveled around Earth three times, reaching speeds of more than 17,000 miles (27,358.9 kilometers) per hour. His three orbits matched the Soviet Union's achievement of orbital flight, accomplished by Gagarin.

Glenn was the first human to see both a sunrise and sunset in space and to take photographs of Earth. Just as the sun came up he witnessed a strange phenomenon that looked like fireflies outside the capsule window. "All around me, as far as I could see, were thousands and thousands of small, luminous particles." Only after a follow-up mission did NASA figure out the mystery of what they were: tiny bits of ice sticking to the outside of the capsule.

How did NASA follow his flight? The U.S. Departments of State and Defense helped NASA set up tracking stations around the world in nations that were aligned with the United States or neutral. Nevertheless, Glenn flew parts of his mission without communication with NASA, while he was out of radio range between tracking stations.

Glenn's capsule splashed down in the Atlantic Ocean and was recovered by U.S. Navy personnel. He returned to a hero's welcome, with parades in Cape Canaveral,

Friendship 7

① NASA WORKERS HELP JOHN GLENN INTO *FRIENDSHIP 7* BEFORE THE LAUNCH.

② ARRIVING IN CEYLON (NOW SRI LANKA) AS A PART OF ITS "FOURTH ORBIT" WORLD TOUR, *FRIENDSHIP 7* IS GREETED BY AN ELEPHANT.

③ PRESIDENT JOHN F. KENNEDY, JOHN GLENN, AND GENERAL LEIGHTON DAVIS RIDE IN A PARADE IN COCOA BEACH, FLORIDA, CELEBRATING THE ASTRONAUT'S FLIGHT.

Florida; Washington, D.C.; and New York City. People admired his courage to do what no American had accomplished before. After the flight Glenn and *Friendship 7* embarked on a three-month world tour to promote the U.S. space program—and U.S. foreign policy interests. He became a national hero and one of the most famous people in the world, inspiring many people with his life story.

This brave man from a small town in Ohio had enlisted in the military during World War II. As a Marine aviator, Glenn flew fifty-nine combat missions in the war and ninety missions in two tours during the Korean War. He then became a test pilot, and in 1957 he flew the first supersonic transcontinental flight. Glenn left NASA in 1964 and eventually ran for public office, serving as a U.S. senator from Ohio. In 1998, at the age of seventy-seven, Glenn returned to space aboard Space Shuttle *Discovery* during the STS-95 mission, becoming the oldest American astronaut.

But it was Glenn's successful orbit of Earth in 1962 that showed the world that the United States was beginning to catch up with spectacular Soviet achievements in the Cold War space race.

MARINER 2

BEFORE MARINER 2, HUMANS HAD BEEN ABLE TO EXPLORE THE SOLAR SYSTEM ONLY BY LOOKING THROUGH TELESCOPES.

Venus had long enchanted them. As the closest planet to Earth, it is a near twin to this planet in terms of size, mass, and gravity. However, a mysterious cloak of clouds permanently hides its surface from view.

Mariner 2, which was launched on August 27, 1962, provided a closer look at Venus. The world's first successful interplanetary spacecraft, it passed within 22,000 miles (35,000 kilometers) of Venus and collected valuable data. It discovered that Venus's surface is extremely hot, making it unlikely that life exists there. And it confirmed that Venus rotates in the opposite direction of the other planets. *Mariner 2* then flew on to orbit the Sun.

Mariner 2 was the first spacecraft to radio scientific information about another planet back to Earth. Its launch inaugurated a series of unpiloted spacecraft missions to other planets and their moons, as well as to asteroids and comets. These probes have added immensely to our knowledge of the solar system and how it formed.

The *Mariner 2* mission was flown in the context of the space race with the Soviet Union. After a number of Soviet firsts, *Mariner 2* gave the United States an important win in the race.

ENGINEERING MODEL OF *MARINER 2* ON DISPLAY AT THE NATIONAL AIR AND SPACE MUSEUM.

What happened to its predecessor, *Mariner 1*? At launch, the Atlas rocket carrying it veered off course, and NASA intentionally destroyed it after only 293 seconds of flight. Upon investigation, engineers found that the fault was a symbol that had been left out of the complex guidance equations. After the error was corrected, *Mariner 2* was successfully launched only thirty-six days later. NASA received data from the satellite for four months.

ASSEMBLY AND BUILDUP OF *MARINER 2* BY ENGINEERS IN HANGAR A&E, CAPE CANAVERAL, FLORIDA.

For many years many people had believed that life could exist on Venus, given its apparent similarity to Earth. But when *Mariner 2* visited, those hopes were dashed. That probe, and later ones, verified that conditions there were too hostile to support life. *Mariner 2* carried instruments to measure heat coming from Venus's surface and atmosphere. They found that the surface, hidden beneath a thick layer of clouds, is extremely hot—800 degrees Fahrenheit (427 degrees Celsius)—with little difference in temperature from day to night. Also unlike Earth, Venus lacks a strong magnetic field to block cosmic radiation.

The satellite's two winglike parts were solar panels. They collected the Sun's energy to power the spacecraft instruments. Its single large directional dish antenna transmitted data to and from Earth. At the distance *Mariner 2* traveled, a large antenna was needed to send detailed scientific data. Other antennas included a smaller omnidirectional antenna on the mast and a smaller one on the end of each solar panel.

Although the *Mariner 2* launch was successful, many later U.S. and Soviet missions to Venus and Mars have failed for various reasons. The exploration of deep space is unforgiving of errors.

AS THIS COMIC BOOK SHOWS, FOR MANY YEARS PEOPLE BELIEVED THAT LIFE COULD EXIST ON VENUS, GIVEN ITS APPARENT SIMILARITY TO EARTH.

LOCKHEED SR-71 BLACKBIRD

THE SLEEK

LOCKHEED SR-71 BLACKBIRD STILL HOLDS THE RECORD AS THE FASTEST JET-PROPELLED BIRD IN THE SKY.

Its ability to fly at speeds of Mach 3 (about 2,000 miles per hour!) and a high altitude of more than 16 miles above Earth (about 85,000 feet!—more than 25 kilometers) allowed it to go deep into enemy territory and avoid interception. Its speed and altitude made it almost invulnerable to the weapons of its day. It could speed up and outrace threats.

Flying at more than three times the speed of sound generates temperatures of 600 degrees Fahrenheit (316 degrees Celsius) on external aircraft surfaces, which is high enough to melt conventional aluminum airframes. That's why the SR-71's external skin was made of titanium alloy (a metal with a melting point of 3,000 degrees Fahrenheit), to shield the internal aluminum airframe. The aircraft skin could withstand heat to about 1,050 degrees Fahrenheit. Because it got so hot, a special paint was used on the outside of the aircraft to help it withstand the high temperatures. The dark blue paint contributed to its name, Blackbird.

Even the aircraft's tires, which retracted into the wings during flight, had to be protected from melting! They were made from latex mixed with aluminum and then filled with nitrogen. The tire pressure on the SR-71 was 415 pounds per square inch (psi)—compared to the 32–35 psi in automobile tires.

A wonder of technology, the Blackbird was one of the first aircraft to include features designed to keep it from being detected by enemies. The shape of the airframe reflected as little transmitted radar energy as possible. In addition, its dark blue paint absorbed radio signals, making it difficult for enemies using radar to detect the airplane. The paint also helped camouflage the aircraft against the night sky. Further, the Blackbird was also the most effective reconnaissance aircraft to fly. It had different methods of capturing information—in fact, it was so sophisticated that it didn't always need to fly over enemy territory or wait until dark to collect information.

LOCKHEED SR-71 BLACKBIRD ON DISPLAY AT THE STEVEN F. UDVAR-HAZY CENTER IN CHANTILLY, VIRGINIA.

A wide array of cameras and sensors in the chine could take photographs and record multiple types of information. The complex systems included optical cameras, near-infrared imaging systems, side-looking radar, advanced synthetic aperture radar, and electronic intelligence-gathering systems. The SR-71 could take pictures of wide strips of land and areas of interest miles away, as well as transmit radio waves sideways from

SR-71 IN FLIGHT, PROBABLY SOMEWHERE OVER THE WESTERN UNITED STATES, CIRCA LATE 1970S.

the aircraft, giving it the freedom to image a target from a greater distance.

In some ways, the Blackbird was the king of the sky. No reconnaissance aircraft in history has flown in more hostile airspace around the world, yet the crew rarely had to worry about danger from enemies. One downside was that because it flew so high, the two crew members, the pilot and a reconnaissance systems officer, had to wear pressure suits similar to those worn by astronauts. The suits would protect them just in case there was a sudden pressure loss in the cabin while at a high altitude.

Only thirty-two Blackbirds were ever made. Buz Carpenter, a Blackbird pilot, described his flying experience: "The aircraft had a heavy control stick (it was hard to move) and powerful acceleration pushed you against the seat during takeoff. Yet, it was a delicate aircraft in that you had to carefully handle the controls at such high speeds. The faster you flew the more sensitive the aircraft became and required more concentration and care."

The Blackbird that is now at the Smithsonian set a new speed record. On its last flight, on March 6, 1990, Lieutenant Colonel Ed Yielding and Lieutenant Colonel Joseph Vida flew from Los Angeles to Washington, D.C., in 1 hour, 4 minutes, 20 seconds, averaging 2,124 miles (3,418 kilometers) per hour! They landed at Washington-Dulles International Airport and turned the airplane over to the Smithsonian; it is on display at the Steven F. Udvar-Hazy Center.

GEMINI IV

BEFORE GEMINI IV,
ALL U.S. ASTRONAUTS TRAVELED IN SPACE LOCKED IN THEIR VEHICLES.

During the *Gemini IV* mission, on June 3, 1965, astronaut Edward H. White became the first American to "walk" in space when he opened the right hatch and floated out of his capsule for twenty-one minutes.

The Gemini program took place in the heat of the space race with the Soviet Union. The Soviets had scored several firsts, including the first space walk, which Alexei Leonov took on March 18, 1965. Three months later the United States responded with Ed White's walk. Although the space walk was only one of several *Gemini IV* mission goals, it was the most dramatic.

Why is it called a "space walk" when astronauts usually use their arms to move around? Maybe it should be a

EDWARD H. WHITE FLOATS ABOVE EARTH, TETHERED TO *GEMINI IV* WITH THE GOLD-COLORED "UMBILICAL CORD" IN HIS LEFT HAND AND A MANEUVERING GUN IN HIS RIGHT HAND.

"space float"! The term may come from an older use of "walking" that simply meant to move about or to travel. The first known use of the term "space walk" was during Ed White's walk. White was tethered to the space capsule by a cord. He used a handheld gas jet device to maneuver himself. He was awed by the experience and didn't want to reenter the capsule. When Mission Control directed him to get back in it, he responded, "I'm coming back in . . . and it's the saddest moment of my life."

All spaceflight requires significant ground support. Beginning with *Gemini IV*, ground control (also called Mission Control) moved from Cape Canaveral, Florida, to the new Mission Control Center in Houston. Known by its call sign, "Houston," that center became the symbol of cool, calm management and problem solving through decades of human spaceflight.

Gemini IV was the second of ten similar spacecraft that each carried two American

TODAY SPACE WALKS ALLOW ASTRONAUTS TO ACCOMPLISH NECESSARY WORK. HERE AN ASTRONAUT WORKS ON THE HUBBLE TELESCOPE.

astronauts in 1965 and 1966. A major part of the space race, the Gemini program provided a critical bridge between the basic one-person Mercury capsules and the sophisticated Apollo missions to the Moon. Gemini astronauts learned how to change orbit, rendezvous and dock with other spacecraft, and walk in space. Gemini was the beginning of practical, work-related spaceflights.

Unlike the Mercury program before it, with its automated pilot system, Gemini astronauts piloted the spacecraft. This enabled more complicated maneuvers in space, including rendezvous and docking. *Gemini VIII*, flown by astronauts Neil Armstrong and Dave Scott, achieved the first docking of two spacecraft in March 1966. All of these were important steps toward the goal of landing humans on the Moon.

To reach that goal, NASA engineers had to try new techniques and learn from successes and failures. Ed White, a Texan, experienced both. After he made national headlines with his space walk, he was scheduled to be part of the first Apollo mission. Tragically, he and his two crewmates—Virgil "Gus" Grissom, the second American

in space (a suborbital flight like Alan Shepard's), and Roger Chaffee—were the first astronauts to die on the job. On January 27, 1967, they got caught in a sudden fire on the launchpad and were not able to escape their capsule. They sacrificed their lives for the dream of space travel.

But White's space walk was a big step toward the dream. It paved the way for many future EVAs (extravehicular activities, the term NASA uses for space walks). These have allowed astronauts to repair satellites, build the International Space Station, and service the Hubble Space Telescope.

❶ *APOLLO 1* CREW (*LEFT TO RIGHT*): VIRGIL "GUS" GRISSOM, ED WHITE, ROGER CHAFFEE.

❷ ED WHITE, SUITED UP.

IMAGINATION
AND THE STAR TREK STARSHIP ENTERPRISE

LONG BEFORE
ANYONE FLEW IN SPACE, THERE WERE
BOOKS, FILMS, AND TELEVISION SHOWS THAT FIRED
THE IMAGINATION OF PEOPLE AROUND THE WORLD.

Books, including *John Carter of Mars* by Edgar Rice Burroughs and *The Martian Chronicles* by Ray Bradbury, as well as TV shows like *Lost in Space* and *Star Trek* helped people to dream about space travel in the future.

In the 1960s, families across the United States turned on the TV to watch the latest adventures of Captain Kirk, Mr. Spock, and the other crew members of the USS *Enterprise*. They'd hear the opening lines of the popular show *Star Trek*: "Space: the final frontier. These are the voyages of the starship *Enterprise*. Its five-year mission: to explore strange new worlds, to seek out new life and new civilizations, to boldly go where no man has gone before."

The starship *Enterprise* was the primary setting for the original *Star Trek* television series, which became

STAR TREK FANS LED A SUCCESSFUL WRITE-IN CAMPAIGN TO NAME THE FIRST SPACE SHUTTLE ORBITER (BUILT FOR APPROACH AND LANDING TESTS) ENTERPRISE, AFTER THE TV SERIES' STARSHIP. HERE, MEMBERS OF THE ORIGINAL STAR TREK TELEVISION CAST JOIN NASA OFFICIALS AT ROLLOUT OF ENTERPRISE, 1976.

popular around the world. The unique shape of the starship, zooming through space, came to represent the future. Matt Jefferies's design of the *Enterprise* needed to look powerful—capable of interstellar travel—so the rear nacelles (compartments to hold the engine) held fictional faster-than-light-speed engines. Jefferies created many concepts for *Star Trek*'s flagship. Imagine the starship *Enterprise* upside down. Producer Gene Roddenberry, the creator of *Star Trek*, made one last change to Jefferies's final design: He flipped it over—and an icon was born. The starship *Enterprise*, conceived initially as the vehicle for one television program, became the ship from which a whole fictional universe of starships have been derived.

The *Enterprise* carried a diverse crew on its fictional adventures. The show's stories addressed real social and political issues of the 1960s. By placing them in a space setting, many *Star Trek* scripts addressed cultural and social concerns, including race relations, gender relationships, urban unrest, and the counterculture.

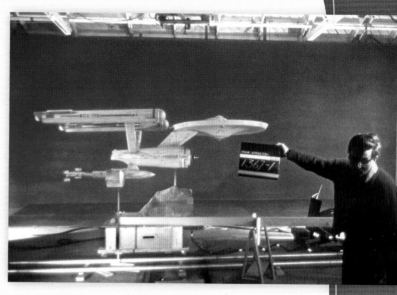

BEFORE COMPUTER-GENERATED IMAGERY (CGI), SHOWING A SPACESHIP IN A MOVIE OR TV PROGRAM MEANT BUILDING AND FILMING A MINIATURE SPACESHIP MODEL. THIS PROP, CIRCA 1966, WAS SHOT ON A STAND IN FRONT OF A BLUE SCREEN (ALLOWING A DIFFERENT BACKGROUND TO BE ADDED LATER). A TRACK WAS USED TO MOVE THE CAMERA, MAKING IT LOOK AS IF THE SHIP WERE ZOOMING THROUGH SPACE.

THE STUDIO MODEL ON DISPLAY AT THE NATIONAL AIR AND SPACE MUSEUM.

Roddenberry's vision of men and women of different races, nationalities, and even species working together aboard the *Enterprise* influenced real spaceflight. Nichelle Nichols played Lieutenant Uhura, one of the first female African American characters on television who wasn't a servant. The civil rights leader Martin Luther King Jr. praised the actress's work on the show and asked her not to leave when she was considering it. In 1977, when NASA wanted a more diverse space shuttle astronaut corps, it hired Nichols to conduct a public awareness campaign encouraging talented people of color and women to apply.

From the original three-season television show, the *Star Trek* universe grew to include additional TV series, major motion pictures, novels, and merchandise. Roddenberry attributed the franchise's success to its hopeful outlook on humanity's future. Most important, many fans of *Star Trek* and other space science fiction franchises now work in fields that are making the dreams of space travel a reality. And they were inspired by the power of television and movies.

NICHELLE NICHOLS, WHO PLAYED *STAR TREK*'S LIEUTENANT UHURA, TALKS TO STUDENTS ABOUT NASA'S SPACE SHUTTLE PROGRAM IN 1977.

LUNAR MODULE AND TOUCHABLE MOON ROCK

THE LUNAR MODULE
(LM) REPRESENTS ONE OF HUMANITY'S GREATEST ACHIEVEMENTS: THE LANDING OF PEOPLE ON ANOTHER HEAVENLY BODY.

It also symbolizes the United States' greatest triumph in its space race with the Soviet Union.

On May 25, 1961, President John F. Kennedy issued a challenge to the American people. He said: "I believe that this nation should commit itself to achieving the goal, before this decade is out, of landing a man on the moon and returning him safely to the earth." His decision followed a series of dramatic first achievements in space by the Soviet Union. Kennedy's advisers suggested that, with a lot of hard work, the United States could show the world that it was able to accomplish something unthinkable at the time. Only three weeks before Kennedy spoke, the country had finally managed to send a man into space, for about fifteen minutes.

As Project Apollo gained steam, many thousands of people across the country worked on various components. Together they contributed to its success. They needed to solve many problems.

ADDRESSING A JOINT SESSION OF CONGRESS, PRESIDENT JOHN F. KENNEDY REQUESTS CONGRESSIONAL SUPPORT TO SEND HUMANS TO THE MOON AND BACK. BEHIND HIM ARE VICE PRESIDENT LYNDON JOHNSON AND SPEAKER OF THE HOUSE SAM RAYBURN.

Engineers had to figure out how to build and launch a rocket that was big enough to reach the Moon. They also needed to decide on the best method for landing on the Moon. What was the best way to train astronauts? What kind of space suit would best protect the astronauts?

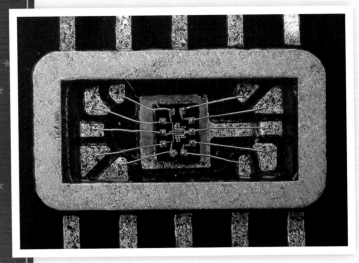

CLOSE-UP OF COMPUTER CHIPS INVENTED FOR THE APOLLO MISSIONS.

THE LUNAR MODULE (LM) WAS DESIGNED TO OPERATE ONLY IN THE VACUUM OF SPACE, SO IT DID NOT NEED AERODYNAMIC SURFACES OR STREAMLINING. IT HARDLY RESEMBLES SPACECRAFT DEPICTED IN MANY SCIENCE-FICTION ACCOUNTS.

In the process, engineers developed new inventions, such as joysticks and cordless tools. Another was the integrated circuit, or silicon "chip." It was designed for the Lunar Module's onboard computer. The astronauts used the computer to guide the LM to a safe landing. Silicon chips did not weigh much and kept the size of the computer small.

Apollo spacecraft carried a crew of three. The LM orbited the Moon joined to a command and service module. The command module remained in orbit with one astronaut, while the other two guided the LM to the Moon's surface (using the LM's lower descent stage) and back (in a separated ascent stage, leaving the lower part on the Moon). All three astronauts returned to Earth in the command module. The rest of the LM was abandoned, to fall out of lunar orbit eventually and crash on the Moon.

The Smithsonian's LM never flew in space. It was built for testing in low Earth orbit but was actually used on Earth

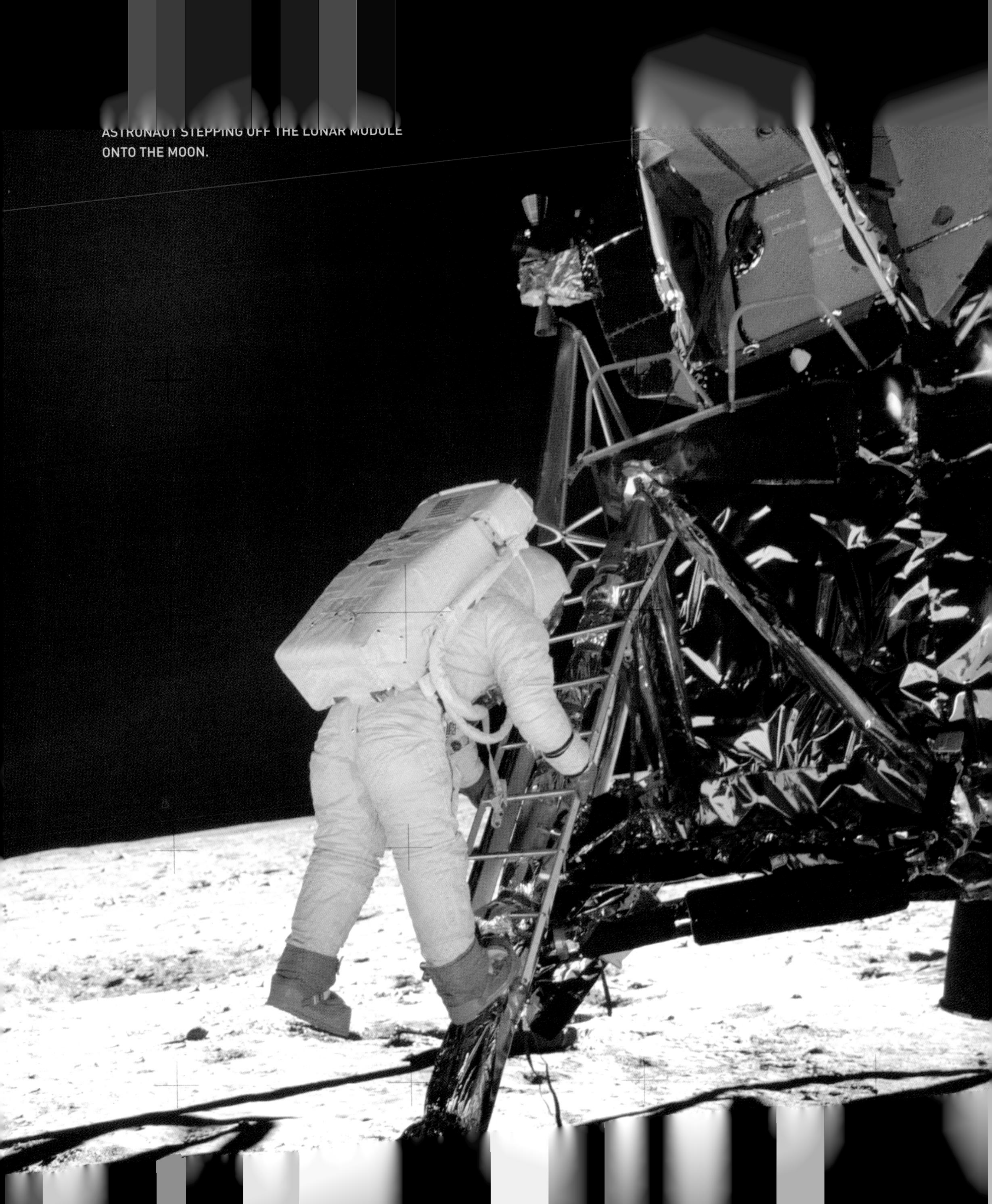

ASTRONAUT STEPPING OFF THE LUNAR MODULE
ONTO THE MOON.

LM IN STARK CONTRAST TO THE DESOLATION OF THE MOON LANDSCAPE.

BOOTPRINT ON MOON

to measure the LM's ability to withstand the forces of landing on the Moon. It is configured to look like *Apollo 11*'s LM, named *Eagle*.

The insect-like LM was designed to operate only in the vacuum of space, so it did not need to be streamlined like a rocket. Its legs are sturdy to withstand a possible hard landing. They include large footpads. Its body is fragile and as light as possible, with a honeycombed aluminum structure. To save weight, it had no seats; the astronauts stood. A thermal blanket of twenty-five layers of high-tech materials protected them.

On July 20, 1969, Neil Armstrong became the first person to set foot on the Moon. He uttered the immortal words: "That's one small step for [a] man, one giant leap for mankind." An estimated 500 million people around the world watched him on television.

In that instant he became one of the most famous people on Earth, just like Charles Lindbergh four decades earlier. Although he held many jobs over his lifetime—naval aviator, aerospace engineer, test pilot, and college professor—Armstrong would forever be known as the first Moonwalker. In his youth Armstrong had earned the rank of Eagle Scout in the Boy Scouts. Among the few personal items that he carried with him to the Moon and back was a World Scout Badge.

Since he was tasked with being the photographer on the Moon, there are only five images of Armstrong on the Moon. The rest show his fellow astronaut, Edwin "Buzz" Aldrin.

Between 1969 and 1972, six Lunar Modules landed a total of twelve American astronauts on the Moon. Since 1972, no human has set foot on the Moon.

TOUCHABLE MOON ROCK

If a person is trying to pack light, the last thing he or she should pack is a bunch of rocks, right? Not if the person is on the Moon and is collecting rocks for people on Earth to study.

The six Apollo missions that landed on the Moon between 1969 and 1972 returned with about 840 pounds (381 kilograms) of rock and soil. Geologists on Earth have studied them to learn about the Moon's history and composition.

In addition to the scientific samples, *Apollo 17* astronaut Harrison "Jack" Schmitt chose one rock to be divided and distributed to foreign governments, the fifty U.S. states, and U.S. territories. This was a smart diplomatic gesture.

❶ ASTRONAUT WITH TOOL AT ROCK.

❷ FULL LUNARSCAPE WITH LARGE ROCK IN FOREGROUND.

❸ HARRISON SCHMITT.

There are only five places in the world where a person can touch a Moon rock: the Kennedy Space Center in Florida; the Johnson Space Center in Houston; the MacMillan Space Centre in Vancouver, Canada; Universidad Nacional Autónoma de México in Mexico City; and the Smithsonian National Air and Space Museum in Washington, D.C. The crew of *Apollo 17*, the last Apollo lunar mission, brought the Smithsonian's rock—sample 70215—back to Earth in December 1972. (The number identifies the mission, the rock's location, and the bag the rock was placed in for return to Earth.) At 17.7 pounds, sample 70215 was the largest rock that the *Apollo 17* crew brought back.

Schmitt was the first scientist to step foot on the Moon and a member of the last crew to visit. He received his PhD in geology from Harvard University and was a rock expert. Before starting his own preparations for going to the Moon, he had served as one of the scientists training the other astronauts. They needed to learn how to be geologic observers and how to know which rocks to collect. After each mission, Schmitt would examine and evaluate the rocks brought back. Imagine how excited he must have been to go to the Moon and do his own collecting!

Because of Schmitt and the other astronauts, millions of people on Earth have been able to look up at the Moon and say they have touched a piece of it. Before the 1960s, the Moon was literally unreachable. Since 1969, people know it's a real destination and that someday it is possible to return.

While still on the Moon, *Apollo 17* mission commander Eugene Cernan remarked that Apollo had opened a challenge for future generations: "The door is now cracked, but the promise of the future lies in the young people, not just in America, but the young people all over the world learning to live and learning to work together."

❶ A VISITOR AT THE NATIONAL AIR AND SPACE MUSEUM TOUCHES A MOON ROCK.

❷ THIS IS THE TOUCHABLE MOON ROCK AFTER IT WAS CUT.

PIONEER 10/11

BEFORE THE TWO
PIONEER SPACECRAFT, NOTHING MADE
BY HUMANS HAD EVER BEEN DESIGNED
TO LEAVE THE SOLAR SYSTEM.

Pioneer 10 and *11* were the first probes to travel beyond the orbit of Mars and cross the solar system's outer reaches. Their mission was to determine whether a spacecraft could travel through the asteroid belt undamaged and also to take the first images of the giant planets Jupiter and Saturn at close range.

Pioneer 10 launched from the Kennedy Space Center in March 1972 and passed the Moon just eleven hours into its flight. Its twin, *Pioneer 11*, launched about a year later. Both traveled through the asteroid belt region between the orbits of Mars and Jupiter without sustaining any damage. *Pioneer 10* transmitted images of Jupiter in late 1973. *Pioneer 11* encountered Jupiter a year later and used that planet's gravity to place itself on a path to Saturn. Five years later it transmitted images of the ringed planet.

Because *Pioneer* kept stable by rotating, it could not focus a camera lens to take photographs as ordinary cameras do. *Pioneer 10* took successive scans of Jupiter as it flew by. These partial images were assembled into one image by astronomers on Earth. The image shows Jupiter's giant Great Red Spot.

The *Pioneer* missions took place immediately after

ARTIST'S DEPICTION OF *PIONEER 10.*

SATELLITE DISH ANTENNA USED TO RECEIVE SIGNALS FROM PIONEER.

the Apollo Moon landings ended. They did not require anywhere near the finances or human effort of Apollo. Yet they generated considerable public interest and support. *Pioneer* and other robotic missions kept alive excitement about space exploration.

The two *Pioneer* spacecraft did not carry a human crew, and their main mission was simply to pass through deep space and collect basic data. But their path out of the solar system did raise an important question: Are we alone?

Astronomers Frank Drake and Carl Sagan and artist Linda Salzman designed a plaque that was fastened to both *Pioneer 10* and *11*. The plaque conveys basic information about the solar system, the spacecraft, and the human beings who built and launched it. It symbolized the hope that an intelligent creature might find it someday as it drifts through the galaxy.

In the 1970s several scientists and space enthusiasts proposed bold new ways to explore space. Gerard O'Neill, a physicist at Princeton University, envisioned a space colony at L-5, a point in space where the gravity of the Sun, Earth, and Moon balance one another. The proposal gained a large degree of support and spawned the L-5 Society, devoted to making the plan a reality. When the very high cost estimates for travel to the location were calculated, however, the idea lost steam.

Last contact with *Pioneer 11* was in 1995. *Pioneer 10* kept traveling. Scientists received a last weak signal from it in January 2003. At that point the spacecraft was 7.6 billion miles (12.2 billion kilometers) away, or eighty-two times the distance between the Sun and Earth. It will coast as silently as a ghost ship into interstellar space, heading generally toward the red star Aldebaran, the eye of the constellation Taurus.

❶ NEARLY FULL-FACE VIEW OF JUPITER MADE BY THE *PIONEER 10* SPACECRAFT FROM 1,842,451 MILES (2,965,000 KILOMETERS) AWAY ON DECEMBER 1, 1974. THE PLANET'S 25,000-MILE-LONG GREAT RED SPOT IS VISIBLE.

❷ ASTRONOMERS FRANK DRAKE AND CARL SAGAN AND ARTIST LINDA SALZMAN DESIGNED THIS PLAQUE, WHICH WAS FASTENED TO BOTH *PIONEERS 10* AND *11*.

VIKING LANDER

FOR CENTURIES
HUMANS HAD SPECULATED THAT THERE MAY
BE LIFE ON MARS. COLORFUL MARTIAN CREATURES
APPEARED THROUGHOUT POPULAR CULTURE.

Science fiction writers told stories of creatures from Mars invading Earth, and even cartoonists created Marvin the Martian to battle Bugs Bunny. In 1976 the *Viking* lander became the first spacecraft to land on the Red Planet and transmit scientific data. The primary goal of the *Viking* missions was to hunt for evidence of present or past life. Some people speculated that there might have been vast civilizations on Mars at one time. While *Viking* instruments detected many of the building blocks of life, they found no conclusive evidence that life ever existed on Mars.

Each *Viking* spacecraft consisted of an orbiter and a lander. The *Viking 1* lander worked for more than six years after landing on July 20, 1976. *Viking 2* landed two months later on the other side of Mars, where it transmitted data for more than three and a half years.

CARL SAGAN STANDS IN FRONT OF A *VIKING* LANDER MOCK-UP IN DEATH VALLEY, CALIFORNIA.

The ability to land a spacecraft and gather data revolutionized what scientists knew about Mars: what it's made of and how it might have formed. And this information offers clues about how our solar system evolved. Each *Viking* lander scooped soil from the surface and deposited it in a miniature robotic chemical laboratory for analysis. *Viking* transmitted dramatic color photos, many showing the Martian sky, which was salmon-colored and not blue, as expected. The landers also measured the wind and sampled the atmosphere.

The Cornell University astronomer Carl Sagan helped select the landing sites and plan the *Viking* missions. He shared his excitement for space exploration with a generation of Americans from the 1970s to the 1990s. Through his PBS television series *Cosmos*, his appearances on such programs as *The Tonight Show* with Johnny Carson, and his engaging writings in popular magazines and books, he helped people to understand the work that scientists were doing.

Viking 1 was a birthday gift to the United States. It landed in 1976, during the 200th-anniversary celebration of

① APPROACHING MARS, *VIKING 1* SENT A SIGNAL TO THE SMITHSONIAN'S NEW NATIONAL AIR AND SPACE MUSEUM (VIA GROUND LINES FROM THE JET PROPULSION LABORATORY IN CALIFORNIA) THAT ACTIVATED A MECHANICAL ARM, WHICH CUT THE RIBBON TO OPEN THE MUSEUM ON JULY 1, 1976, AS PRESIDENT GERALD FORD LOOKED ON.

② MANY OF THE DRAMATIC COLOR PHOTOS TRANSMITTED BY VIKING SHOWED THAT THE MARTIAN SKY IS UNEXPECTEDLY SALMON-COLORED, NOT BLUE. THE LANDERS ALSO ANALYZED THE SOIL, MEASURED THE WIND, AND SAMPLED THE ATMOSPHERE.

American independence. A signal from a *Viking* orbiter cut the ribbon to open the Smithsonian's new National Air and Space Museum on July 1, 1976, as part of the Bicentennial festivities.

Since *Viking*, various robotic rovers have explored the Martian surface, including *Sojourner*, *Spirit*, *Opportunity*, and *Curiosity*. Mars is the only known planet that is inhabited exclusively by robots! In the summer of 2015 there were two active robots exploring the planet. An additional five landers or rovers are there, although not operating. The current Martian activity focuses on finding evidence for past life on the planet. Landers and rovers have discovered evidence of water and helped to prepare us for possible human exploration of Mars. Will humans ever reach Mars? Numerous technical and medical hurdles must be overcome for humans to voyage there. Nevertheless, as helpful as robots are, a human expedition to Mars could accomplish as much science in a few days as *Viking* accomplished in months.

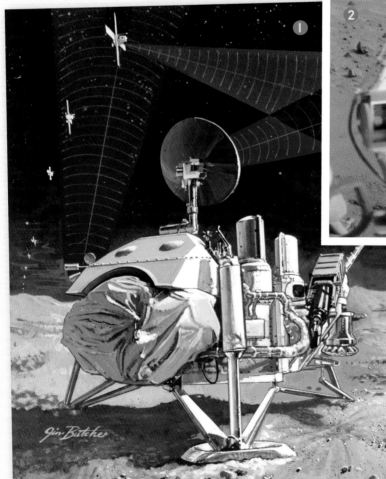

1 THIS ILLUSTRATION OF A *VIKING* LANDER ON MARS SHOWS HOW ITS ACCOMPANYING ORBITER BEAMED DATA BACK TO EARTH.

2 EACH *VIKING* LANDER ANALYZED SOIL FROM THE MARTIAN SURFACE AFTER SCOOPING IT UP AND PLACING IT IN A MINIATURE ROBOTIC CHEMICAL LABORATORY.

SPACE SHUTTLE DISCOVERY

QUESTION:

WHAT LAUNCHES LIKE A ROCKET
AND LANDS LIKE A GLIDER? ANSWER:
THE SPACE SHUTTLE.

FINAL LAUNCH OF SPACE SHUTTLE
DISCOVERY, FEBRUARY 24, 2011.

After the Apollo Moon missions, the United States' goals in space changed. People wanted to stay closer to Earth and not spend as much money. In early 1972, eleven months before the final lunar mission, President Richard M. Nixon made an announcement: "I have decided today that the United States should proceed at once with the development of an entirely new type of space transportation system . . . It will revolutionize transportation into near space, by routinizing it. It will take the astronomical costs out of astronautics."

The workhorse for this new era would be a winged spaceplane that could land on a runway and fly again. The new Space Shuttle program was designed to make access to space less expensive and more routine. It included a manned orbiter and two solid-propellant booster rockets, all reusable. For thirty years (1981–2011) the shuttle fleet served as America's sole vehicle for human spaceflight. Intended to replace expendable launch vehicles that are used only once to send people or cargo into space, the Space Shuttle was the world's first reusable spacecraft.

The Space Shuttle was the most complex space vehicle ever built. Its liquid-propellant main engines were the most sophisticated rocket engines ever constructed. The solid rocket boosters were the largest and most powerful ever flown.

To meet the goal of routine spaceflight, shuttles had to be readied to fly over and over. At any time, a workforce equivalent to the population of a sizable town took care of each shuttle in space and on the ground. They tended it from drawing board to shop floor to launchpad, and from landing to launching, again and again.

People across the United States worked on the Space Shuttle program. Team members at 640 NASA and contractor facilities used more than 900,000 pieces of equipment valued at almost $20 billion. For example, the engines were made in California; the

DISCOVERY ARRIVES AT THE STEVEN F. UDVAR-HAZY CENTER, APRIL 19, 2012.

space suits in Connecticut, with parts from Delaware; the solid-fuel booster rockets in Utah; the external fuel tank in Louisiana; and the turbo pumps in Florida.

The Space Shuttle combined features of a rocket, a spacecraft, and a glider. No other flying machine launched into space served as both a crew habitat and a cargo carrier, maneuvered about in orbit, and then returned from space to land on a runway—again and again.

In 135 Space Shuttle missions, astronauts delivered and retrieved satellites, serviced the Hubble Space Telescope, launched scientific probes, conducted laboratory research, and carried out construction, resupply, and crew exchanges for the International Space Station.

Before the Space Shuttle era, all astronauts were men. Almost all were military test pilots. One was a scientist. Only one, who died in a training accident before he could fly in space, was African American. The civil rights and women's movements in the 1960s and 1970s set the stage for breaking race and gender barriers in spaceflight. NASA actively recruited women and members of minority groups to become Space Shuttle astronauts. In addition, almost fifty astronauts from other nations flew on shuttle missions. Even a member of royalty flew on the shuttle: In 1985, Prince Sultan Salman Abdulaziz Al-Saud joined the crew on a weeklong mission to deploy an Arabsat communications satellite. He was a member of the Saudi royal family, a government official, and a pilot in the Royal Saudi Air Force.

For thirty years, the Space Shuttle proved a capable transportation system, but its cost and complexity remained controversial. The goal of truly routine spaceflight went unfulfilled.

Two orbiters and crews were lost in terrible tragedies. After the second loss—

Columbia in 2003 (the first was *Challenger* in 1986)—the nation's leaders decided to retire the Space Shuttle and redirect NASA's human spaceflight mission beyond Earth orbit. After completion of the International Space Station, the three remaining orbiters landed for the last time. The United States retired the Space Shuttle in 2011.

NASA announced that Space Shuttle *Discovery*, the oldest in the fleet, would go to the Smithsonian National Air and Space Museum. The orbiter's journey to the Smithsonian ended with a spectacular flyover of the Washington, D.C., area mounted on the back of the Boeing 747 Shuttle Carrier Aircraft.

Discovery flew thirty-nine missions over twenty-seven years, from 1984 to 2011. Operating in the range of 115 to 400 miles above Earth, it spent a cumulative 365 days in space—an entire year! The orbiter's primary mission in the 1990s was to support science. It carried observatories, satellites, and laboratories for scientific research. Thirteen of *Discovery*'s last missions went to building the International Space Station. *Discovery*'s diverse crew included the first female shuttle pilot, first female commander, first African American commander, and astronauts from ten countries.

Discovery is now on display at the National Air and Space Museum's Steven F. Udvar-Hazy Center in Chantilly, Virginia. Millions of visitors have come to see it and stand under its wings.

❶ SPACE SHUTTLE *DISCOVERY* ON DISPLAY AT THE STEVEN F. UDVAR-HAZY CENTER, CHANTILLY, VIRGINIA.

❷ NOSE OF *DISCOVERY*, SHOWING THE TILES MAKING UP THE SPACE SHUTTLE'S THERMAL PROTECTION SYSTEM.

HUBBLE SPACE TELESCOPE

MANY SPACE INSTRUMENTS OVER THE YEARS HAVE BEEN DESIGNED TO OBSERVE ACTIVITY ON EARTH. OTHERS, CALLED SPACE OBSERVATORIES, LOOK IN THE OPPOSITE DIRECTION, INTO OUTER SPACE.

While many of these have allowed us to gather new information about our universe, there is one that has profoundly changed the way we see the world beyond our solar system. NASA's Hubble Space Telescope (HST) was released into Earth orbit in 1990 from Space Shuttle *Discovery*. It has sent back to Earth mesmerizing images of distant galaxies and stars being born, of black holes and stellar clouds, and of the surface of Pluto.

HUBBLE HERITAGE PROJECT IMAGE (ILLUSTRATION) DEPICTING A GRAZING ENCOUNTER BETWEEN TWO SPIRAL GALAXIES; IT WAS CREATED FROM THREE SEPARATE "POINTINGS" OF HUBBLE USING ITS WIDE FIELD PLANETARY CAMERA.

Telescopes on Earth are located on tall mountains so as to be free of pollution as much as possible. But their view is still not as clear as the Hubble's. The HST orbits about 350 miles above Earth. This allows astronomers to see the universe unhindered by the ocean of air we live in, which blurs and distorts our view of the heavens. Building a high-quality telescope on Earth is expensive, but space telescopes are very expensive, too. In fact, the Hubble is the most expensive astronomical telescope in history. While the idea of a telescope in space was proposed as far back as 1923, the history of the Hubble can be traced to 1946, when an American astronomer named Lyman Spitzer wrote a paper calling for a space telescope.

It was a long process, but eventually the telescope was completed. Officials named it for Edwin P. Hubble, an American astronomer who in the 1920s discovered galaxies beyond our Milky Way and who first measured the universe's expansion rate.

For the Hubble's designers, the biggest challenge was not building the telescope or even launching it into space.

ATTACHED TO THE ROBOT ARM, THE HUBBLE SPACE TELESCOPE IS REMOVED FROM ITS BERTH AND LIFTED UP INTO THE SUNLIGHT DURING THE SECOND SERVICING MISSION.

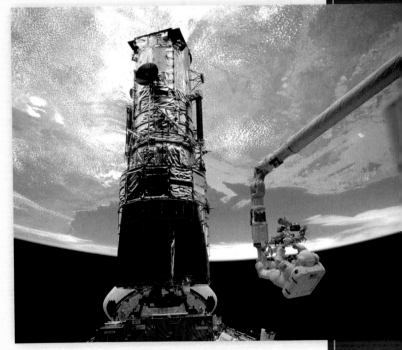

THE 1993 SERVICING MISSION WAS THE FIRST OF FIVE TO UPGRADE THE HUBBLE SPACE TELESCOPE. ASTRONAUT STORY MUSGRAVE WORKS ON IT FROM THE SPACE SHUTTLE'S ROBOTIC CANADARM.

The challenge was how to capture the data that the telescope gathered and send it to Earth. Once its engineers solved this, they were ready to go. They built the telescope so it could be carried to space aboard Space Shuttle *Discovery*. The astronauts deployed it in space, and the world waited for the images it would send.

But astronomers quickly realized that there was a problem: The images they were receiving were blurry. After some investigation, they concluded that the telescope's primary mirror was flawed. The Hubble had to be fixed. Fortunately, the HST had been designed so that astronauts could service it in space. It took two and half years, but finally, in 1993, NASA sent astronauts up on the Space Shuttle to repair the Hubble. They removed one of the telescope's instruments and replaced it with a device that reversed the primary mirror's flaw. The Hubble was not only repaired but improved. Astronaut crews flew to service it four more times before the Space Shuttle program ended. The HST continues to detect even more distant and younger objects in the universe.

The Hubble's public impact has been huge. People around the world have gazed in wonder at its images. Their appreciation for the expansive universe is greater because of Hubble. The Hubble telescope is the most popular space observatory, and since it has been operating, astronomers have written thousands of scientific papers based upon its observations.

The Hubble continues to send vivid images back to Earth, allowing astronomers to learn new information about our universe.

A VIEW OF THE HUBBLE SPACE TELESCOPE FROM INSIDE THE SPACE SHUTTLE ATLANTIS IN 2009.

SPACESHIPONE

PEOPLE HAVE
LONG DREAMED OF BUYING A TICKET FOR A FLIGHT INTO SPACE.

Even before the first astronauts set foot on the Moon, 93,000 people had joined a waiting list for a "First Moon Flights" club with Pan American World Airways. Pan American had hoped to begin flights in 2000. But this never happened—and Pan Am is no longer in business.

An American entrepreneur, Peter Diamandis, founded the X Prize Foundation in 1995 to inspire space development in the way that the Orteig Prize, won by Charles Lindbergh in 1927, spurred the airline industry. He agreed to give $10 million to the person or company that developed a space vehicle capable of carrying three people into suborbital spaceflight—up to 62 miles (100 kilometers)—and repeating the feat within two weeks.

In 2004 a privately built, piloted craft named SpaceShipOne—designed by Burt Rutan and financed by Paul Allen— won the prize. (It was renamed the Ansari X Prize for the Iranian American business partners Anousheh and Amir Ansari.) SpaceShipOne reached space and returned safely. Its success inspired the creation of Virgin Galactic,

AMIR AND ANOUSHEH ANSARI, WHO FUNDED THE ANSARI X PRIZE, WITH PETER DIAMANDIS (*RIGHT*).

91

SPACESHIPONE AT
THE NATIONAL AIR
AND SPACE MUSEUM.

a company founded to offer private suborbital flights in space to tourists. It also helped clear the way for NASA's public-private partnerships to develop new spacecraft to carry crews and cargo to the International Space Station.

Before SpaceShipOne won the Ansari X Prize, there was no privately developed and operated way to go into space. Since then, several firms have developed spacecraft for different kinds of commercial space travel.

How did SpaceShipOne work? A larger aircraft called the White Knight carried it to launch altitude. Upon release, SpaceShipOne's rocket engine powered it into space. When it reached top altitude, it tipped over for a smoother, more efficient reentry. Its jointed wings pivoted into a "feathered" position to steady its flight back into the atmosphere, much like a badminton shuttlecock.

Anousheh Ansari fulfilled her own long-held dream in 2006 when she made a private spaceflight. She traveled to the International Space Station via a Russian Soyuz spacecraft, a trip brokered by Space Adventures, Ltd. Since 2001 seven private citizens have each paid a lot of money for the opportunity to go into space with the Russian government-run space program.

Many people hope that someday they will be able to travel into space and maybe even live there. The dream is closer to reality because of SpaceShipOne.

A LARGER AIRCRAFT, WHITE KNIGHT, TRANSPORTED SPACESHIPONE TO LAUNCH ALTITUDE. WHEN IT WAS RELEASED, SPACESHIPONE'S ROCKET ENGINE POWERED IT INTO SPACE.

EPILOGUE

WHAT IS THE NEXT

MILESTONE IN FLIGHT? IT'S HARD TO IMAGINE
A TIME WHEN THERE WERE NO AIRPLANES.
IN THE FUTURE IT MAY BE HARD TO IMAGINE A TIME
WHEN PEOPLE DON'T HAVE ACCESS TO SPACE TRAVEL.

In the span of less than a hundred years, Earthbound humans built machines to fly across oceans ... and then to the Moon ... and then to deep space.

People will always invent and innovate and find new ways and better ways. Sometimes an idea will work; sometimes it won't. Sometimes an idea works only on a small scale, and sometimes it transforms all of society. Many times ideas require a great deal of resources, both financial and human. Sometimes these resources are available, but sometimes they aren't.

Will airplanes get faster, or hold more people? Will humans finally reach Mars or land on an asteroid? Will we return to the Moon? Will new satellites and telescopes bring us information that changes the way we look at the universe? What surprises are around the corner?

No one can predict the future. But as Wilbur and Orville Wright, Robert Goddard, Neil Armstrong, Gene Roddenberry, and many other people around the world have already demonstrated, a curious mind, a desire to learn, and big dreams will lead to the next milestones of flight and transform the world.

DETAIL FROM ROBERT McCALL'S LARGE MURAL *A COSMIC VIEW*, LOCATED IN THE SOUTH LOBBY OF THE MUSEUM.

GLOSSARY

biplane: an airplane with two sets of wings, usually one above the other

chine: on certain airplanes like the SR-71 Blackbird, a flared part that runs from the nose to the wing and forms an edge, which helps provide additional lift and control at very high speeds

Cold War: a state of political and military tension between countries of the Eastern bloc, led by the Soviet Union, and the Western bloc, led by the United States and its allies—less a physical war than a war of ideas

commercial aviation: the business of flying goods and passengers

drone: common name for a UAV, an unmanned, or unpiloted, aerial vehicle

drop launch: raising a vehicle, usually a test vehicle, to a certain altitude and then launching it by dropping it into the air

flyby: when a robotic spacecraft flies past a planetary body but does not land

flying boat: a plane that landed on water

geostationary: a circular orbit above Earth's equator that follows the rotation of the planet; also called geosynchronous

glider: an aircraft without an engine; unlike a powered aircraft, which uses an engine to generate thrust or power to move forward, a glider must be launched from a hill or towed aloft by another airplane until it is released, after which it relies on altitude and gravity to generate the speed to move forward, like a vehicle coasting downhill

hypersonic: highly supersonic, speeds of Mach 5 (five times the speed of sound) and above; heat becomes a critical factor

jet engine: an engine in which a very strong stream of hot air and gases blast from the rear to propel the vehicle forward

lander: a vehicle that lands on a planetary body but does not change location

NACA/NASA: the National Advisory Committee for Aeronautics (NACA), a federal agency in the United States founded in 1915 to undertake and promote aeronautical research, it became the National Aeronautics and Space Administration (NASA), to combine aeronautical and space-related research, in 1958

orbit: to travel around something (such as Earth) in a curved path

piston engine: one that uses moving parts called pistons to transfer energy

propellant: a substance that provides or causes propulsion in a rocket; the fuel in a rocket

propeller: a spinning wing (usually with the help of an engine) that produces lift, like a wing, but in a forward direction, using rotary motion through the air to create a difference in air pressure between the front and back surfaces of its blades

radar: an object-detection system that uses *radio waves* to determine the range, altitude, direction, or speed of objects rover: a vehicle for exploring the surface of a planetary body

satellite: an object (such as the Moon) that moves around a much larger planet; also a human-made object designed to orbit Earth and transmit data of various kinds

Soviet Union: officially, the Union of Soviet Socialist Republics (USSR), a country that existed from 1922 to 1991 and comprised fifteen different countries (called republics), the largest and most dominant of which was Russia

supersonic: exceeding the speed of sound, Mach 1

transonic: about Mach 0.8 to Mach 1.2; air is flowing faster than sound over some parts of the airplane

TIME LINE

1783 Montgolfier brothers launch the first hot-air balloon flight with human passengers.

1793 The first balloon flight in the United States takes place.

1861 Thaddeus Lowe demonstrates the use of a balloon for President Abraham Lincoln.

1876 The Smithsonian collects its first flight object, a Chinese kite.

1903 Wilbur and Orville Wright fly the first airplane at Kitty Hawk, North Carolina.

1909 Glenn Curtiss wins a race at the world's first international air meet, in France.

1914–18 **WORLD WAR I**

1914 The world's first scheduled airline begins service in Florida.

1916 The Curtiss JN-4 goes into service.

1918 The U.S. Post Office Department makes the first official delivery of airmail.

1919 KLM, the Dutch airline, begins passenger service; it is still flying today.

1924 The crews of Douglas World Cruisers complete the first flight around the world.

1926 Robert Goddard launches the world's first liquid-fuel rocket.

1927 Charles Lindbergh is the first pilot to fly solo across the Atlantic Ocean, from New York to Paris, without any stops.

1931 The National Advisory Committee for Aeronautics (NACA) builds the world's largest wind tunnel, in Virginia.

1935 The Douglas DC-3 first flies.

1937 Sir Frank Whittle becomes the first to successfully test a jet engine.

1939 Hans Pabst von Ohain's jet engine becomes the first one to fly.

1939–45 **WORLD WAR II**

1941 Radioplane delivers the mass-produced OQ-2 drone to the U.S. Army.

1942 The XP-59A Airacomet flies for the first time.

1947 The Bell X-1 breaks the so-called sound barrier.

1947-91 **THE COLD WAR**

1954 The Boeing 367-80 flies for the first time.

1957 The Soviet Union launches *Sputnik 1*, the world's first human-made satellite.

1957-72 The space race between the Soviet Union and the United States

1958 The United States launches its first satellite, *Explorer 1*.

1959 The X-15 first flies.

1960 *The Discoverer XIII* becomes the first human-made object retrieved from space and the United States' first reconnaissance satellite.

APRIL 1961 Soviet cosmonaut Yuri Gagarin is the first human in space and in orbit around Earth.

MAY 1961 Astronaut Alan Shepard becomes the first American in space.

MAY 1961 President John F. Kennedy addresses Congress and proposes a program to put a man on the Moon.

1962 The world's first active communications satellite, Telstar, is launched.

FEBRUARY 1962 Astronaut John Glenn becomes the first American to orbit the Earth.

1962 *Mariner 2* becomes the world's first successful interplanetary spacecraft.

1964 The first flight of the SR-71 Blackbird, the fastest jet-propelled aircraft, takes place.

MARCH 1965 Cosmonaut Alexei Leonov completes the world's first space walk.

JUNE 1965 Astronaut Edward H. White becomes the first American to complete a space walk.

1966 The TV series *Star Trek* first airs on American television.

1967 NASA loses three astronauts in a tragic fire.

1969 Astronaut Neil Armstrong becomes the first person to walk on the Moon.

1972 The final Apollo mission goes to the Moon.

1972 *Pioneer 10* launches, the first probe into the outer reaches of the solar system.

1972 President Richard M. Nixon announces the space shuttle program.

1976 *Viking* becomes the first spacecraft to land on Mars and transmit scientific data.

1981-2011 The Space Shuttle fleet operates.

1984 President Ronald Reagan authorizes NASA to construct an international space station.

1990 The Hubble Space Telescope is deployed.

2004 SpaceShipOne wins the Ansari X Prize.

2011 The last mission of Space Shuttle *Discovery* is completed, marking an end to the space shuttle program after thirty years.

ENDNOTES

MILESTONE 1

The Montgolfier brothers experimented with tethered flights in October 1783. But the November 21, 1783, flight of Jean-François Pilâtre de Rozier and François Laurent, the marquis d'Arlandes, was the first manned free flight in history.

MILESTONE 2

"It is not uncommon...": http://airandspace.si.edu/exhibitions/wright-brothers/online/who/1895/biketoflight.cfm.

MILESTONE 5

"New Rocket Devised...": *Boston Herald*, January 20, 1920.

"A Severe Strain on Credulity": *New York Times*, January 13, 1920.

"Hopes to Reach Moon...": *New York Times*, May 25, 1924.

MILESTONE 6

"What kind of man...": Von Hardesty, *Lindbergh: Flight's Enigmatic Hero* (New York: Harcourt, 2002), 71.

MILESTONE 11

"the only pilot...": General Chuck Yeager and Leo Janos, *Yeager: An Autobiography* (New York: Bantam Books, 1985), 126.

"I realized that...": Yeager and Janos, *Yeager*, 165.

MILESTONE 13

"This ball will...": https://airandspace.si.edu/exhibitions/milestones-of-flight/online/current-objects/1957.cfm.

"Never before had...": Daniel J. Boorstin, *The Americans: The Democratic Experience* (New York: Random House, 1973), 591.

MILESTONE 14

"the most successful...": http://www.seattlepi.com/local/article/Famed-aviator-Scott-Crossfield-dies-in-plane-crash-1201589.php.

MILESTONE 15

"We've spent $35 or $40 billion ...": Jeffrey T. Richelson, *America's Secret Eyes in Space: The U.S. Keyhole Spy Satellite Program* (New York: Harper & Row, 1990), 93.

MILESTONE 16

"It was only ": Michael J. Neufeld, ed., *Milestones of Space: Eleven Iconic Objects from the Smithsonian National Air and Space Museum* (Minneapolis: Zenith Press, 2014), 30–31.

"a rapid development...": Neufeld, *Milestones of Space*, 26.

MILESTONE 17

"All around me...": Neufeld, *Milestones of Space*, 13.

MILESTONE 19

"The aircraft had . . .": https://airandspace
.si.edu/events/techquest/past-missions/eye-
in-the-sky/blackbird.cfm.

MILESTONE 20

"I'm coming back . . .": http://www.jsc.nasa
.gov/history/mission_trans/gemini4.htm.

MILESTONE 22

"I believe that . . .": President John F.
Kennedy, address before a joint session of
Congress, May 25, 1961, https://www.nasa.gov/
vision/space/features/jfk_speech_text.html.

"That's one small step . . .": http://www
.hq.nasa.gov/alsj/a11/a11.html.

"The door is now . . .": http://www.hq.nasa
.gov/alsj/a17/a17.html.

MILESTONE 25

"I have decided today . . .": http://history
.nasa.gov/stsnixon.htm.

BIBLIOGRAPHY

Many of the pioneers highlighted in this book have written autobiographies. There isn't space to list them all here. I encourage young readers to read these primary sources.

BOOKS

Carl, Ann B. *A WASP Among Eagles: A Woman Military Test Pilot in World War II.* Washington, D.C.: Smithsonian Institution Press, 2010.

Clary, David A. *Rocket Man: Robert H. Goddard and the Birth of the Space Age.* New York: Hyperion, 2003.

Grove, Tim. *First Flight Around the World: The Adventures of the American Fliers Who Won the Race.* New York: Abrams, 2015.

Hardesty, Von. *Lindbergh: Flight's Enigmatic Hero.* New York: Harcourt, 2002.

Neufeld, Michael J., ed. *Milestones of Space: Eleven Iconic Objects from the Smithsonian National Air and Space Museum.* Minneapolis: Zenith Press, 2014.

Van der Linden, F. Robert, ed. *Best of the National Air and Space Museum.* Washington, D.C.: Smithsonian Books, 2006.

Yeager, General Chuck, and Leo Janos. *Yeager: An Autobiography.* New York: Bantam Books, 1985.

BLOG POST

Anderson, John D. "The NACA/NASA Full Scale Wind Tunnel." http://blog.nasm
.si.edu/history/full-scale-wind-tunnel.

WEBSITES

National Air and Space Museum, *America by Air* exhibition, http://airandspace.si.edu/exhibitions/america-by-air/online.

National Air and Space Museum, *Wright Brothers* exhibition, http://airandspace.si.edu/exhibitions/wright-brothers/online.

National Air and Space Museum, *How Things Fly* exhibition, http://howthingsfly.si.edu.

ACKNOWLEDGMENTS

Any book project is a team effort. This book is based in large part on the exhibition script for the Boeing Milestones of Flight Hall written by museum curators Robert van der Linden, Margaret Weitekamp, Paul Ceruzzi, and Alex Spencer, with input from the author and the rest of the exhibition team. Parts of Milestone 25, about space shuttle *Discovery*, were adapted from the *Moving Beyond Earth* exhibition script sections written by Valerie Neal and Roger Launius. I'm privileged to work with some of the world's experts on aviation and space history and am grateful for review from the following colleagues at the Smithsonian National Air and Space Museum: John D. Anderson Jr., Roger Connor, Tom Crouch, David DeVorkin, Michael Hulslander, Peter Jakab, Maureen Kerr, Michael Neufeld, Bob van der Linden, and Margaret Weitekamp. My intern, Kate Oltersdorf, provided help at a critical time and deserves much thanks, as does Tom Paone for his excellent photo research and the National Air and Space Museum Archives staff for their ongoing help. Finally, thanks to editor Howard Reeves and the other staff at Abrams who provided generous support, insight, and encouragement along the way.

ILLUSTRATION CREDITS

p. 2: Courtesy of the Smithsonian Libraries; p. 7: Smithsonian Institution Archives Image # SIA2014-05379; p. 13: National Postal Museum; pp. 24, 25, 26: NASA/Langley Research Center; p. 29: Rudy Arnold Photo Collection, Smithsonian National Air and Space Museum; p. 34 (*right*): Draganfly Innovations; pp. 35, 36 (*top*): U.S. Air Force; p. 51 (*bottom*): National Park Service; p. 53 (*top*): Center for the Study of National Reconnaissance, National Reconnaissance Office; p. 56: AT&T; p. 63: Used with the acknowledgement of the Frank R. Paul Estate; p. 66: Lockheed Martin Corporation via Smithsonian National Air and Space Museum; p. 71 (*top*): Courtesy of Curt McAloney and Dave Tilotta; p. 80 (*top*): NASA/JPL-Caltech; p. 88: photo by NASA and Hubble Heritage Team, Smithsonian National Air and Space Museum; p. 91: Jim Campbell for XPRIZE Foundation; p. 92 (*bottom*): XPRIZE Foundation; pp. 47, 48, 49, 50, 60, 67, 68, 69, 70, 72, 73, 74, 75, 76, 77, 78 (*bottom*), 79, 81, 82 (*bottom*), 83, 84, 85, 88, 89: NASA. All other images are public domain or are used by permission of the National Air and Space Museum. The work of the following National Air and Space Museum photographers is featured in this book: Mark Avino, Richard Hofmeister, Eric Long, Dane Penland, and Carolyn Russo.

INDEX

Note: Page numbers in *italics* refer to illustrations.